Archives

The very essence of our heritage

Archives

The very essence of our heritage

Christopher Kitching
for the National Council on Archives

Phillimore

1996

Published by
PHILLIMORE & CO. LTD.
Shopwyke Manor Barn, Chichester, West Sussex

© National Council on Archives, 1996

ISBN 1 86077 018 5

Printed and bound in Great Britain by
LAWRENCE-ALLEN LTD
Weston-super-Mare, Avon

Contents

Acknowledgements

This book draws heavily on the collective knowledge and experience of the organisations which together make up the National Council on Archives, as described more fully in the Appendix. I am grateful to all those who supplied information or suggested illustrative material. It was possible to include only a selection, and the choice is very largely a personal one.

The Council is grateful to its member organisations for financial and practical support in the preparation of this book, and to the Department of National Heritage in underwriting some of the production costs. It is especially grateful to the many repositories and individuals who generously supplied photographs for the illustrations, and in every case agreed to waive their usual reproduction fees in order to lend tangible support to the publication. The illustrations are reproduced by courtesy and kind permission of the respective organisations and individuals accredited in the list of illustrations at the end of the volume, whose copyright where applicable is gratefully acknowledged.

Colleagues too numerous to mention, at the Royal Commission on Historical Manuscripts and on the National Council on Archives, commented on the text in draft. With their enthusiastic and critical encouragement it has been a real pleasure to act as compiler of this volume on behalf of the National Council on Archives.

CHRISTOPHER KITCHING
August 1995

1 Paper repair at Birmingham City Archives

Archives
and what they mean to us

'Archives, which contain the primary record of our past, are the very essence of our heritage'

(Viscount St Davids)

'A nation must be judged on how it conserves its archives. Our future depends on our past and we must make sure that it is always available'

(Lord Montagu of Beaulieu)

These telling points were made during the Parliamentary debates in 1993 and 1994 about local government in England, Wales and Scotland, amid fears that proposals for its restructuring could unintentionally jeopardise our archives and archive services. Other speakers acknowledged that the United Kingdom was 'amazingly rich' in ancient documents, which were 'unique and irreplaceable', 'the repository of family and local history', 'reflecting all aspects of the life and times of communities'; and that these were 'not only for historians but also for citizens who need access to information concerning their own affairs'.[1]

In this book, the National Council on Archives takes up those themes, in order to share with a wider public that sense of the grandeur but also the accessibility of our archival heritage. The text and the pictures illustrate the diversity both of the archives themselves and of the uses to which they are put, the partnerships that have evolved to provide for their care and exploitation, and the responsibilities attached to these tasks.

What are 'archives'?

'Archives', in the popular sense of the word, can be almost any historic documents. Quite commonly they are also called 'records', although this term also covers items which are still in daily use: to distinguish those from the historic material we sometimes call them modern or current records. Nevertheless the terms 'record office' and 'record repository', just as much as 'archives office' or 'archives centre', have come to be used of places for the public custody of archives. The archives which they hold, however, are in fact an assemblage of many separate 'archives' in a different sense of the word, namely the documentation created and/or accumulated respectively by many people or institutions in the course of their daily life and work and retained in perpetuity because of its lasting importance.

Today this documentation might be represented partly in photographs, audio-tape or film, or in a computer-readable medium, as well as on paper. It is not the form or medium that dictates whether or not a particular item is of archival significance, but its context: in particular its 'provenance', or link with the creator of the archive. Nor is age necessarily a factor: archives can be of very recent origin. Nor, finally, are archives solely the product of the official activities of bodies such as central or local government: they are generated by organisations of all kinds (businesses, the churches, schools, charities, learned bodies and so on), and by individuals and families. As Sir Cyril Flower said in 1946 when introducing the newly-founded National Register of Archives to a public audience, 'You may read a letter at the breakfast table and say to yourself, "I will keep this". You are creating an archive'.

'For citizens who need access to information'

In many walks of life, archives – both public and private – are needed on a daily basis as the source of information about actions taken or decisions recorded in the past which continue to affect our rights and entitlements today.

Registers of births, marriages, deaths or adoptions, for example, help to establish our very identity, our ancestry and birthright. Title deeds contain evidence of individuals' rights to real estate, or of the age of a building and the succession of its ownership. Charters define corporate rights and privileges. Trust deeds spell out, for example, the terms of reference of a charity. Patents for designs and inventions protect commercial interests. Architects' drawings of a country house or garden which are often to be seen exhibited, for example in the National Trust's houses, may be aesthetically pleasing in their own right but they assume a vital new rôle when it comes to restoring the interior to its original colours or returning the garden to its original design. Businesses may recycle designs from the historic labels, posters or artwork in their archives for today's packaging or advertising. Maps and plans can have many practical uses, from establishing or verifying rights-of-way to identifying old mine workings which might cause building subsidence, contaminated land which might be a hazard to future generations, the lines of drains or the structure of buildings.

Just as this newsletter was being written, a house in Lonsdale Street, Elton, was completely demolished by a gas explosion, apparently caused by gas leaking up a small culvert or drain from a broken main over a hundred yards away. A researcher from British Gas has already been round to try and trace the background of this particular hole. Other people have consulted us over subsidence affecting property, methane gas leakage from old rubbish tips, flooding from culverts and sewers, and possible pollution from old waste dumps.

Bury Archive Service Newsletter
for April/May 1994

We may need practical information of this kind as a matter of urgency. Indeed, in some record offices legal and business searches have become an industry in their own right.

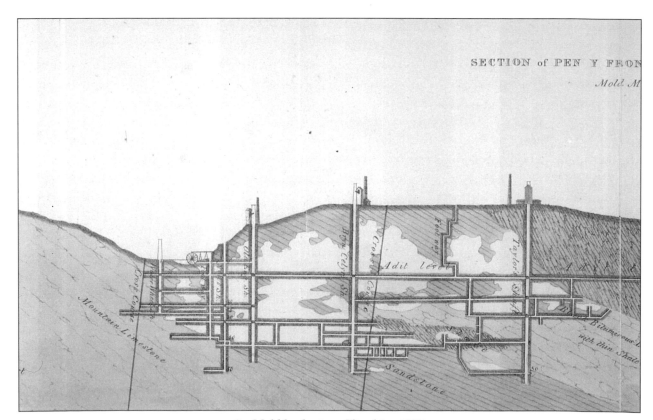

2   Mold lead mines, Flintshire, 1827

3 Stafford waterworks: trial sinking at Milford, 1892

The history of our communities

At national level archives are the key to an understanding of past governmental policies and decisions which have affected every sphere of life, in both domestic and foreign policy. We are reminded of this each January as the press eagerly descends upon the Public Records newly released under the thirty-year rule.

But archives serve a wider cultural need. They provide a framework for our understanding of the past: how our forbears thought and behaved, what life was like for them; how they worked and played; the social, religious or political context of their lives. At the level of the local community they can help to explain how a building, a street, a village or a town, or for that matter a business or other organisation, took shape and why it is as it is now.

They can hold the answer to particular puzzles of local history. It would be hard to think of a better embodiment of Olde Englande than Winkle Street at Calbourne on the Isle of Wight with its stream and thatched cottages. At one point the watercourse is impeded by a stone structure. A plaque nearby announces that the survey of the manor of Swaynston in 1640 and the Tithe Commissioners' survey of 1842 show that it was a sheepwash.

On a wider plane, the work of Derek Keene and others has shown how evidence assembled systematically from title deeds and the like can build up a history of site occupancy for whole streets and towns in our ancient cities such as Winchester and London, which can then be used to complement archaeological evidence. Historical geographers too are combing records for evidence of historical land use, settlement patterns and the development of placenames.[2]

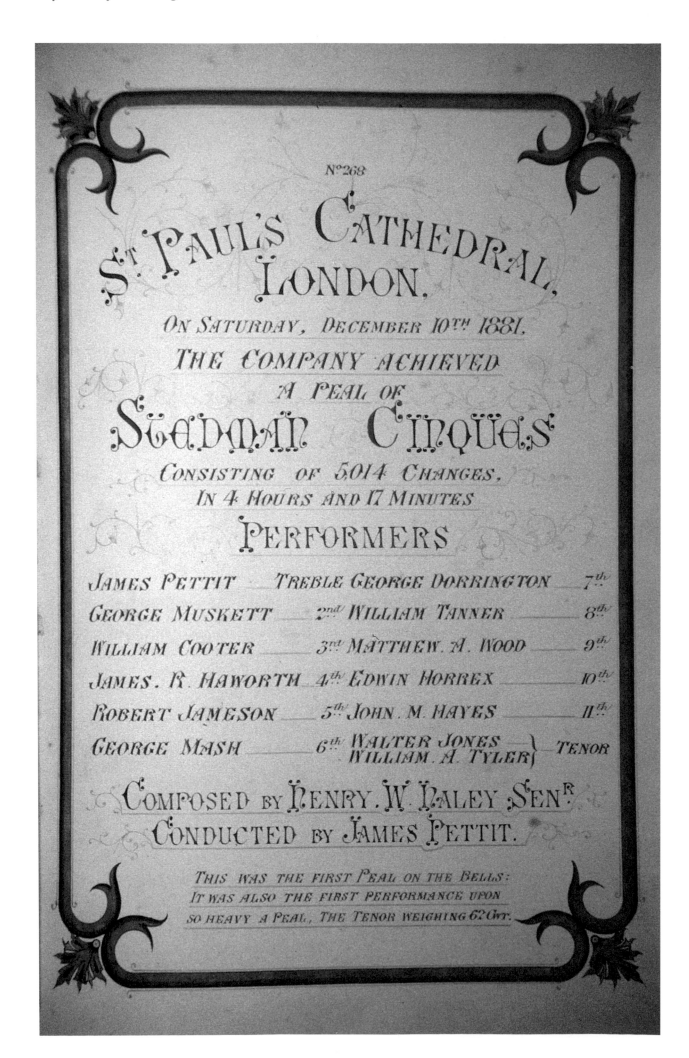

No. 268

St Paul's Cathedral, London.

On Saturday, December 10th 1881.

The Company Achieved

A Peal of

Stadman Cinques

Consisting of 5,014 Changes,
In 4 Hours and 17 Minutes

Performers

James Pettit	Treble	George Dorrington	7th
George Muskett	2nd	William Tanner	8th
William Cooter	3rd	Matthew. A. Wood	9th
James. R. Haworth	4th	Edwin Horrex	10th
Robert Jameson	5th	John. M. Hayes	11th
George Mash	6th	Walter Jones / William. A. Tyler	Tenor

Composed by Henry. W. Haley. Senr.
Conducted by James Pettit.

This was the first peal on the bells:
It was also the first performance upon
so heavy a peal, the Tenor weighing 62 Cwt.

5   James Melville's diary, 1574 with the first known archival reference to golf

Archives as a national and international resource

The records of individual government departments, of local communities, or of individual families or businesses, studied in isolation, may tell us quite a lot about their respective originators. When made available for study alongside other comparable records they achieve as it were a 'critical mass' that can sustain wider research, whether of a local, national or even international character. It would be quite wrong to assume that British archives were of interest only to British readers, or indeed that any body of archives was exclusively of interest to one narrow constituency. The National Register of Archives was consulted in 1993-94 by people from every continent, in all from some thirty countries. And the international interest in British archives extends well beyond the national repositories. West Glamorgan County Archive Service, in Swansea, for example, reported enquiries and visits during 1994-95 from Europe, Turkey, the Middle East, South Africa, New Zealand and the USA.[3]

In the aftermath of the fire at Norwich Central Library in August 1994, it was feared (wrongly, as it happened) that many of the local records had been destroyed. Scholars from Oxford and Tel Aviv wrote to *The Guardian* on 8 August:

These records have proved a goldmine for a wide range of scholars with interests in drama, popular culture, health and medicine, historical epidemiology, demography, social policy, immigration, nutrition and diet, household structure, family history and occupational analysis. There are many questions which only Norwich records can answer.

If we multiply that conclusion by the number of record repositories and accessible private archives around the country we can see that the potential of our archives as a whole for sustaining research is enormous.

The increasing availability of archives for study has undeniably broadened the kind of research that can be undertaken. This is not only because more evidence makes for better-informed research, but also because familiarity with a wider range of records and the data they contain has helped historians and others to know where to turn for evidence that was previously thought to be in acutely short supply, for example for the study of women or children in the Middle Ages or of ethnic communities in recent times.

A good deal of advanced research of course transcends the limits not just of individual archives but of individual repositories too. Ronald Hutton's recent survey entitled *The rise and fall of Merry England*[4] drew together information from the surviving churchwardens' accounts for three centuries from all over England and Wales. Nicholas Rodger's biography of John Montagu (1718-1792), 4th Earl of Sandwich,[5] was based not only on the Sandwich papers now in the National Maritime Museum, but also on many other official records and private papers there as well as in the Public Record Office (PRO), and the British Library; and private papers in the PRO of Northern Ireland, three university collections, five county record offices, the Royal Archives and six private houses in England, Scotland and Guernsey, two research libraries in the United States and the Royal Archives of the Netherlands.

With the help of the National Registers of Archives (*see p. 34*) scholars can now identify even the most far-flung sources. A glance at the Registers also quickly warns us against thinking that everything of national importance will be found in a national repository or everything of local importance in a local one. Ted Rowlands MP claimed in the Parliamentary debate already mentioned that 'the finest collection of letters [and] account books ... of the birth of the world's industrial revolution' was the Dowlais letter books in Glamorgan Record Office. We shall see below something of the national and international significance of the holdings of local authority record offices and university and specialist libraries.

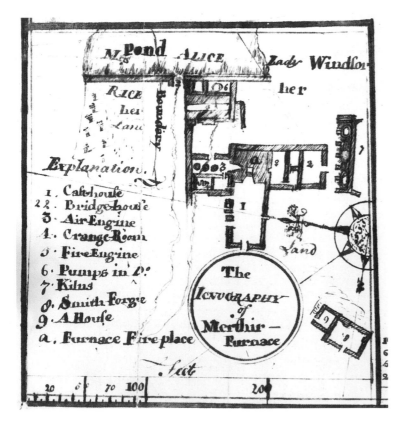

6 'The icnography of Merthir Furnace', 1763 from the Dowlais Iron Company archive

7 Denbigh charter, 1510

Archives as evidence

The evidential nature of archives has been recognised from the earliest times.

This has led to strenuous efforts to keep safe all proofs of rights and entitlements, from the enrolment of copies of documents in the official records of courts of law to the enshrinement of the American Declaration of Independence in a container filled with inert gas in the National Archives in Washington DC. On the other hand it has also led adversaries throughout recorded history deliberately to attack and destroy archives which might establish their opponents' territorial or civil rights or conversely contain evidence against the attackers themselves. William the Conqueror's devastation of the north of England in 1069 included the burning of some of York Minster's archives. Rioters in 1757 forced Sir Roger Burgoyne to hand over the militia lists for Biggleswade, Bedfordshire, 'fearing that if they were enlisted they would be forced to serve overseas'. Bolton cotton spinners in 1823 seized records of their Combination, which might have been used against them. Among a number of more modern examples, it was reported that Georgian troops in 1992 burnt the national archives of Abkhazia.[6]

Archives have often been demanded as evidence in courts of law, usually in civil cases to determine some right or entitlement such as an inheritance or perhaps commons or mineral rights, or proof of identity. Less commonly they have featured in criminal cases. Staffordshire Archives Service's annual report for 1993 recorded how bricks used as ransom demand markers by a kidnapper had been shown by forensic tests to have been manufactured at a tilery whose order books were preserved in the Record Office. The police used the archives to locate stockpiled supplies of the bricks, which eventually led them to make an arrest.

8 Grant of arms to the Coach and Coach Harness Makers' Company, 1677

The thrill of discovery

For most researchers, discoveries among the archives are much less dramatic, and the consequences less far-reaching than that. But the same sense of satisfaction, even thrill, is experienced by researchers coming across just the piece of evidence they have been looking for, whether it was the missing link in the family tree, the first recorded reference to the making of ice-cream, the text of a hitherto unknown poem or play or music score by a renowned author or composer, or something to support the theory that Napoleon Bonaparte died from poisoning.

Occasionally it still falls to archivists, researchers and even private citizens to make startling discoveries of documents nobody had dreamt still existed, like the extremely rare leaf from the 6th-7th century Ceolfrith Bible, found in 1982 being used as a wrapper for 16th-century muniments at Kingston Lacy, Dorset; the fragment of a medieval world map found in the binding of a volume in the Duchy of Cornwall archives; the 14th- and 15th-century deeds for the foundation of chantries in St Michael Spurriergate, York, brought in to York University's Borthwick Institute of Historical Research in April 1995 by children, after its discovery during alterations to their school; or the bakers' account book 1784-1841 covering a number of Bedfordshire villages, again found in the course of building alterations and donated to the county record office in 1971.[7]

Perhaps it should be added that no lesser satisfaction awaits researchers who discover material which has been freely available for generations but has remained unread or unrecognised.

Archives in context

Such discoveries often depend first on a knowledge of the context in which the records themselves were created and then on the particular questions asked of the sources to hand, because different researchers asking different questions will put the same archives to quite different uses.

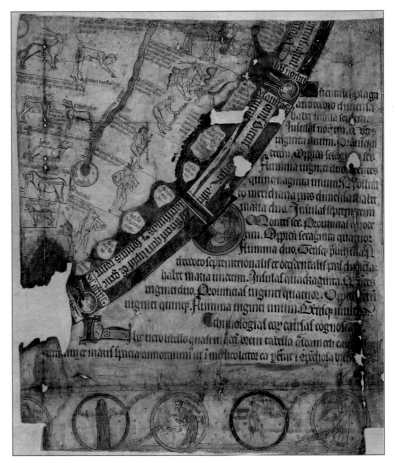

9   Fragment of a medieval world map, *c.*1220, discovered in the binding of a volume in the archives of the Duchy of Cornwall

In compiling lists of archival material, archivists seek wherever possible to explain the context in which the archives were created, drawing on internal information from the archives themselves as they sort and describe them, but also on external information such as published biographies, directories and company or organisational histories. It is this contextual approach, and also the fact that the very great majority of archives are unique and irreplaceable, that distinguishes them from printed library resources, and produces systems of indexing and classifying quite different from those used by librarians. Almost all researchers will have to use both library and archival sources, but those turning to the archives will need to realise that they cannot always, as with printed books, simply look up an author, a title or a subject. More deliberate detective work is required to get to the heart of the archival evidence.

Archivists seek to respect the evidential nature of the archives in their care. As far as possible they keep together the archives of any one individual, family or institution, and do not mix them up with those of any other. And if they can discern it they keep the constituent units in the order in which they accumulated or were used by the creator/generator of the archive. So they would not normally rearrange letters by their subject matter if they had been kept chronologically or by correspondent. Nor, for example, would they separate out items that were specifically of postal history interest because of the stamps or frankings on their envelopes. This is the difference between the archivist on the one hand and the collector or dealer on the other, who may tend to think of each item separately and iconically and be more interested in the way it exemplifies one particular theme or genre.

Promoting access and use of archives

'The value of an archive,' said Lord Elton,[8] 'is its accessibility.' To put this another way, we have not really appropriated our archival heritage at all until we have access to it.

Many record repositories have long been working hard at public outreach, through lectures, group visits, publications and exhibitions, and through roadshows and other public events taking archives to the heart of the community. As a direct result archives in the United Kingdom have never had more friends than they do today, as more and more people find if not a professional then a leisure-time interest in studying the past; as the utility of archives for research in many disciplines is becoming better recognised; and as access to primary source material for the study of history is increasingly being demanded at all levels of our educational system.

One good reason for using original archival sources in the study of history is that the evidence has to be carefully assessed against a knowledge of the context in which it was created: why and by whom the information was recorded in the

10   Family history day at Huddersfield

11   Young historians' day at Sheffield

12   Pedigree roll of the Gwyn family of Llansannor, Glamorgan, *c.*1615

first place; why it was recorded in that way; whether it represents incontrovertible fact, or the writer's opinion or preconception, or perhaps even a deliberate attempt to deceive.

More and more archive services are responding to the need for access to primary materials in education: by producing copy packs or publications of documents, by employing professional education officers or encouraging teachers to bring parties of children or students to the record office. Archives of every kind can be successfully exploited if careful preparatory work is done by both archivist and teacher. To take just one example, the Bass brewery archives have been put to good educational use, to reveal the everyday life of the company and its work-force as shown in employee records, accident reports, letters and indentures, foremen's

standing orders or sports and social club minutes; and the history of the town of Burton-upon-Trent, illustrated through photographs, estate and valuation records, architects' drawings and maps of the brewery railway. Special studies have been built on the company's wartime records, and at tertiary level the archives have been exploited to support studies in marketing, advertising, business studies and art and design.[9]

Something like a million visitors per year pass through the doors of our publicly-funded record offices and other archive-holding institutions throughout the country. A modest proportion are full-time academics, research students, professional writers, or those needing access to records for legal or business purposes. Nor should we underestimate the appreciable administrative use made of their own deposited historic records

13   Hearth tax money collected in Lochrutton parish, Kirkcudbrightshire, 1694

(4)

The par[oc]hin of Lo[ch]rutton	fearths	lib	ß.
Imp: The Laird of Auchenfrankow — —	009	06:	06
Item the Laird of Drummore — — — — —	001	00	014
Item the Laird of hills — — — — —	030	18 —	18
grof thrie poor beggers			
Item the Laird of Carsnadda — — — —	009	04	18
grof two beggers			
Item Bogrow — — — — — — —	003	02	02
Item James Williamson in houghinland John			
McCaurspie William Miller — — —	003 —	02	02
Item Nether barfill — — — — — —	002	01	08
Item Langtoune — above — e — under the			
Brae — — — — — — —	004	02	16
Under the Brae of Carsnadda — — — —	002	001	08
Item Nunlands interof twinke grof			
thrie beggers — — — — — —	020	ij.	18.
Item Barnburscell — — — — — —	006	04	04
Item Maondell Barfill — — — — —	002	01	08
Item Barnhar 7 grof one and begger	006	04	04
Item Drantoune one — — — — — —	001	00	14.
John Hoggart	098	63	04
		63	00
The parochin of Terrbyles			
Imp: within the place of Terrbyles — — —	015.	10	10
Item My Lord Nithsdaill interof — — —	026	18	04
laty the house			
Item the Kirkland Thomsone interof ye	005	02	16
grof one and begger			
Item the Collodye — — — — — — —	10	30	10
Jno Hoggar	56	38	10

14   The search room at Canterbury cathedral archives

by the agencies of central and local government themselves. But by far the majority of users are citizens (as well as an increasing number of overseas visitors) engaged in family or local history.

There is still a need to raise the level of general awareness about the work that is being done – and still needs to be done – to preserve our written heritage. When public expenditure is tightly restrained there always seem to be other priorities. And no doubt there are sceptics who still share what was once Lord Hertford's view of archives as 'doing nothing, gathering dust'.[10] Why spend public money on acquiring them, and then more still on preserving them, making them available and housing them properly? This volume is dedicated to the doubters just as much as to the converted. Without strong public support, little progress can be made towards achieving the objectives for our archives that were so thoughtfully set out in those Parliamentary debates.

An Incomparable Written Heritage

Our archives are among the richest and most comprehensive in the world. They sustain research from Anglo-Saxon times to the present, in every branch of knowledge for which a historical perspective is helpful, whether in the arts, the humanities or the sciences.

It would be cheering to report that the survival of these rich resources was due to a rooted national conviction that the care of our archives is a measure of our civilisation itself. That view lay behind the high-Victorian idealism that created, for example, the Public Record Office and the Historical Manuscripts Commission. But it has all but vanished today.

To be blunt, we owe our archival heritage to:
* good luck (the limited incidence of invasion and civil war in these islands compared with other European countries; our temperate climate; our freedom from disasters, ranging from termite invasion to earthquakes, which have widely befallen archives elsewhere);
* benign neglect in earlier generations; and, only thirdly,
* the determined efforts of some individuals and the goodwill of many more.

Some of our records extend in unbroken series from the 12th and 13th centuries. They therefore provide a solid foundation for writing our national and local history. Extremely important individual items survive from earlier centuries, like the Anglo-Saxon charters or Domesday Book itself (1086).

Archives now lost

On the other hand, a great deal has also been lost or scattered.

In a few cases this has been through deliberate and malevolent destruction, or as a side-effect of more general property confiscations, for example at the time of the dissolution of the religious houses in the 16th century or the Jacobite risings in the eighteenth.

The full sense of our loss may be glimpsed from the rich series of monastic archives which did survive intact for a number of the former monasteries which escaped demolition, such as Durham cathedral or Westminster abbey. Not all were so fortunate. Dr Rodney Thompson's catalogue of *The archives of Bury St Edmunds*[11] identified major groups of former Bury muniments not only in the PRO and British Library but also in Suffolk Record Office, the Bodleian Library at Oxford, and among the Bacon family papers in the University of Chicago Library. Others had found their way into the University Library at Cambridge, the libraries of various Oxford and Cambridge colleges, the borough archives of King's Lynn, the county record offices of Hertfordshire and Warwickshire, Lambeth Palace Library and Westminster Abbey muniment room, as well as to the Pierpont Morgan Library in New York and the Bibliothèque de la Ville in Douai.

Losses have also occurred through the migration of records in troubled times. First in the 1290s and again in 1650 the English made off with some of the Public Records of Scotland and failed to return them intact. More spectacularly in the latter case, some were lost at sea during an attempted repatriation.[12] Fires and floods too have taken their toll, in houses,

15 The first Winchester Pipe Roll, 1208-09

churches and business premises. Fire, for example, destroyed important Welsh family archives at Wynnstay, Raglan and Hafod.[13] More widespread losses resulted from the Great Fire of London in 1666 and the fire of 1922 in Dublin Castle which destroyed most of the Public Records of Ireland, dating from the early 12th century, and with them nearly half the pre-1870 parish registers of the Church of Ireland.

Godfrey Davis's survey of *Medieval Cartularies of Great Britain*[14] notes examples of cartularies destroyed in fires at Birmingham Central Library and Staple Inn, in the Great Fire of London and the fire in the Cottonian Library in 1731; another was lost when Wardour Castle (Wiltshire) was destroyed during the Civil War, and from yet another only a few pages were rescued from children's drumheads made at Exeter.

Highest among the causes of archival losses, both historically and nowadays, must surely be neglect by their owners or custodians, often arising from an unawareness of the archives' wider cultural value. Archives have been put aside for further thought on a 'rainy day' that somehow never came, in attics and cellars, boiler rooms and even bathrooms, stable blocks and garden sheds – anywhere that space could be found. Sadly, this applied even to many of the records of state in England until at least the mid-19th century. The medieval writ files of the Court of King's Bench were excavated from under a pile of builders' rubble in the Public Record Office as recently as the 1970s. How many times this tale could be retold around the country for the papers of businesses, corporations and private individuals. Sometimes the owners were lucky in their choice of storage space, finding adequate shelter and a stable, cool and dry environment, and the archives then survived benign neglect. More often they were unlucky, and the archives were exposed to assault from rats and insects, damp and mould, leaking roofs or smoking chimneys and the polluted atmosphere of urban and industrial areas. Spare a thought for the heroic local historians of Lymington (Hampshire), who in the 1970s had to excavate parish records buried beneath household refuse on the corporation rubbish tip.[15]

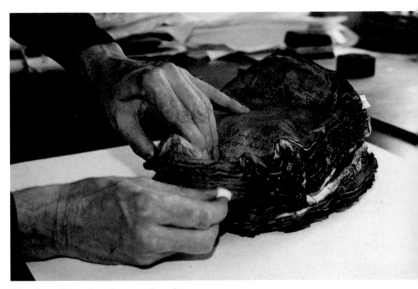

16   Repairing fire damaged archives

Further losses have commonly occurred at moments of family or business upheaval: the death of their owner leading to their sale or destruction by the grieving relict; a removal to new premises by a family or business leading to a 'good spring-clean', with archives going wholesale into the skip or off to the shredder. At various times they have been sold or given to waste paper merchants, to tradesmen as wrapping paper, to bookbinders as end-papers, or used domestically to make lamp-shades or even to serve as bungs in wine casks. This is not the kind of utility we wish to encourage!

The Second World War brought significant losses, with the salvage drive for paper, the requisitioning of country houses for the billeting of troops, and some direct destruction through aerial bombardment, as in the case of the Exeter probate records. But one happy side-effect was a heightening of public awareness of the need to take specific steps to protect archives and make them better known. One result was the establishment of National Registers of Archives, in London (for the whole of the UK) and in Edinburgh (for Scotland) to locate records and papers of historical importance. And in turn, particularly in England and Wales, this contributed to the flowering of local record repositories that we have witnessed in the last half century.

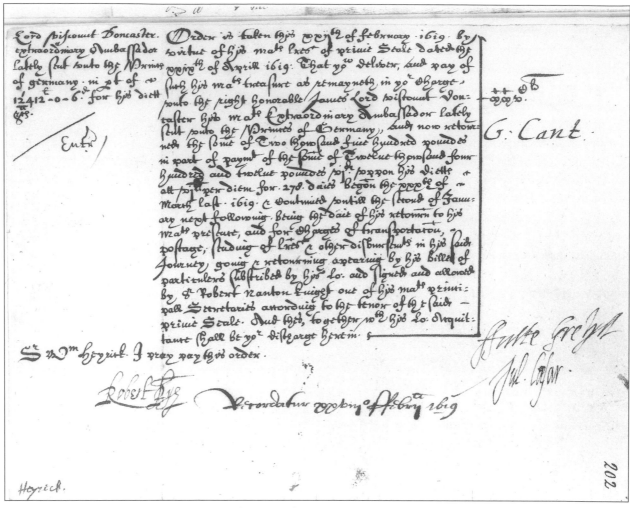

17   Official papers of Sir William Herrick (1562-1653), teller of the Exchequer, now in the Bodleian Library Oxford

Strays

Some archives that might at first be thought lost have merely come to rest in an unexpected place. It is important to grasp that our network of record repositories is, in historical terms, a very recent development. In earlier generations, for want of adequate controls over any but the most frequently used records and those of the central courts, it was normal even for the great officers of state to retain most of their official papers at home. The same habit spread quite widely among officials in organisations of all kinds – colleges and universities, courts of law, charities, even parishes – and it was not unknown for a retiring official or perhaps his widow to sell the records to the successor in office as a perk. As a result, many official records are now to be found among private papers, only some of which are in public custody. Many of the papers of Elizabeth I's chief minister, William Cecil, Lord Burghley (1520-1598), for example, remain in family possession at Hatfield House, whilst some of the papers of another of her ministers, Sir Nicholas Bacon (1509-1579), are now in the University of Chicago Library.

Archives migrate or go to ground for a variety of other reasons. Families and estates unite by marriage; businesses merge or are taken over; charities and pressure groups move to new premises or change name to project a different image; and so on. It is the researcher with persistence and lateral thinking who is most often rewarded.

18   High Commission Act Book, 1631-33, now in Cambridge University Library

Tertia Sessio Termini Trin: | Jovis die

...prox̄i prox̄imo p̄imo mensis Junij Anno Dñi 1632 coram venerabilibus in xp̄o p̄ribus et dñis Georgio providentia divina Cantuariensi Archiepō, Guilino London, Theophilo Menduce et Johe Rossen eadem providentia... Epis, legvariis Marten Arnold Cesar, Johe Lambe et Nathanaele Brent militibus, et legum Doctoribus, Henrico Parker legum Doctore, Decano de Arcubus Arnte, et Roberto Aylet legum Doctore, Commissionarijs Regijs ad causas Ecclesiasticas apud Lambehith indicialiter sedent, coram Thoma Motershed Registrarij Regij deputato...

Officium dñorum contra Paulinum Woode de Chessham in Com: Buchs yed D Synod, D Dudl, Gwess

Ad audiend̄ pro tam quoad taxationem expensarum... In die dñi assignament ad idem in proxi touchinge the taxation of Expences... And there where was a petition given upp by him for the Mitigation of the fyne and for his enlargment which was rejected by the Court.

Officium dñorum contra Arthure Taylor de Sutton in Com: Chester, D Bennett, D wood, gers Whetstone

This day the order sur sentence of the Court sett downe the last Court day was opposed and appealed against by the Councell of the sayd Taylor, but the same being read in open Court, was confirmed and ratified by the Court and the fyne of D li imposed uppon him was adiudged to be imposed by the Court. And the said Taylor is to purge him selfe before the first Court day of the next Tearme and to be enlarged uppon bond given to performe the order of the Court.

Officium dñorum contra Arthure Whitacres militis Baronet, D Ryves, Gers

Mr Dr̄ Ryves insisteth on his admonition... it is to appeare this day... This day he appeared personally and judicially admonished from henceforth not to print, or cause to be imprinted hereafter any booke whatsoever without sufficient license or warrant first obtayned, and soe was dismissed, payinge the Charges of the Court.

Officium dñorum contra Robertum Baxter, Martinum Lucas et Robertum Constable par̄ Sc̄e Anne Blackfryers

They were ordered to put in their defence this day. They are to sweare ar. Additionally and then to put in a defence if they will, and soe the Cause to goe on in an ordinary course.

Officium dñorum contra Edwinu̅ Russell et alios de Cheshunt in Com Hurtf, D Ryves

Ad audiend̄ pro tam insit plene p̄xm... This day the Register was required by the Court to examine the p̄ces and to be sure to take their answeres fully to the fact within the tyme estat.

Officium dñorum contra Mission Sparke Baronet, D Ryves Gwm Colo, Gers

This Day Mr Colo Proctor for the office gave in an allegacon and exhibitte and desired to have the same admitted but the Councell for the Deft opposed that... and alledged that the same ought not by law to be admitted whereupon it was referred to Sr Henry Marten to admitt or reject the same pro hac vice.

1874

Week ending. Oct 16th 1874

This school was opened on Monday as a Public Elementary School. The necessity of its opening was fully shewn by the large number of children who presented themselves for admission, nearly 100 children being present on the first day. The children shew a strong desire to improve themselves. their education having been greatly neglected. The greater part of this week has been occupied in putting the children into their proper classes, but it has been accomplished, and next week. I hope to commence work in earnest. The school was visited during the week by Rev W. Griffiths, Mrs Griffiths and several others, who expressed their pleasure at seeing so many children present.

Henry Meek. Master

Oct 23rd

Admitted 15 children this week. A fair week's work has been done by the children. I have prepared a Time Table which I intend to put into operation as soon as possible. Revs Walter Griffiths and Hughes visited the schools during the week.

19 Log book of Tonna Mixed School, Glamorgan, 1874

Survey and rescue

At national level both the Royal Commission on Historical Manuscripts and the National Register of Archives (Scotland) undertake systematic surveys of records of national importance and offer advice to owners on their care or disposition. In addition a number of voluntary or charitable bodies and research centres are dedicated to the survey and rescue of archives. The **Records Preservation Section** of the **British Records Association**, for example, has since 1928 acted as an agent finding suitable homes in public repositories throughout the country for unwanted and in some cases forgotten records, from the offices of London solicitors in particular but also from businesses and individuals. The Section's work has brought to light not only an immense quantity of title deeds but also important holdings of manorial and estate records and impressive individual documents of national as well as local importance. As recently as 1992/93 the Section found stray Stuart state papers, thought to have been kept by Charles II's secretary while in exile in the Hague, which were forwarded to the Bodleian Library in Oxford to be under the same roof as the Clarendon Papers.[16]

In the field of business, both the **Business Archives Council** (BAC) and its Scottish counterpart, **BAC Scotland**, have long track records of conducting surveys of business archives and steering them into safe custody in repositories.

> *Only those who have themselves donned a boilersuit, worn a face-mask and worked for hours (sometimes with the aid of a torch) listing the hundredweights of dust-laden records that frequently comprise a large collection of business records can fully appreciate the magnitude of their achievement.[17]*

A number of central research institutions conduct surveys in other special fields. They include the **Contemporary Medical Archives Centre** at the Wellcome Institute for the History of Medicine and the **National Cataloguing Unit for the Archives of Contemporary Scientists** at the University of Bath. The Wellcome Institute and the PRO have joined together to survey

20   Pedigree of Lord Selsey discovered by the British Records Association

hospital records, and maintain a database giving locations. Many local record offices keep an ear to the ground for archives in need of rescue, although with an eye on the costs of this work they may have to concentrate at any one time on particular surveys, for example of business, educational or church records. Some have insufficient resources to undertake survey work directly, but almost all offer advice free of charge if approached.

Archivists respond to the most difficult and even dangerous challenges in order to rescue records. The **Hampshire Archives Trust** was

21   A solicitor's basement in the early 1980s

the first organisation of its kind, set up independently but as a surveying arm of a county record office, to survey and locate records throughout the county and to offer advice to their owners.

> *Access to the upper floor...was by a broken ladder. The view of the upper room from the top of the ladder was unforgettable. Piles of ledgers, mounds of documents several feet high, maps...Any disturbance of the material caused choking clouds of black dust to rise. Additional hazards were quantities of broken glass and what appeared to be decayed boxes of garden chemicals.[18]*

We should all be the beneficiaries if more individuals and institutions came to see the wider cultural value of their archives and entrusted them to professional care at an earlier stage.

Partners in the Care of Archives

22   Aerial view of Hampshire Record Office, Winchester

Archive services: a network of care

Statutory provision is made in the United Kingdom only for the custody of the records of government and a few other specific categories of records which, although not defined as 'Public Records', are of continuing legal or financial significance. These include manorial and tithe documents in England and Wales, the records of the established (or formerly established) Churches, the records of local authorities, and some records of companies.[19]

There has never been any central body in the UK to determine where, when or by whom new record repositories should be established. But, partly in response to administrative necessity, academic interest or the wider public conscience of the respective stakeholders, there has been a steady growth over the past half-century in the number of repositories established to take in archives, preserve them, and at the right time make them accessible for public consultation. As explained more fully below, these are funded respectively by central and local government, the universities, businesses and sometimes by private initiative.

The lack of any central control means among other things that in the UK – as indeed in most other countries – there is a degree of competition for custody of the available archives. But on the whole the spread of professional training and of national standards for the care of archives has meant that the different kinds of repository have learnt to live together and to recognise that they do in fact form something like a 'network' for the protection of the written heritage, and that this is worth fighting to preserve and if possible improve. Their partnership is an underlying theme of this book.

With very few exceptions public repositories in the United Kingdom – which are listed in the directory *Record Repositories in Great Britain* published periodically by the Historical Manuscripts Commission – currently provide a free service and admit every *bona fide* researcher on an equal basis to study all archives which are at present open to research. As a general rule, government records are statutorily closed to public inspection for a minimum of thirty years. Similar closure periods are quite widely applied in other repositories, although greater restrictions – fifty years or more – apply everywhere in the case of archives that contain nationally sensitive material or private or commercial information obtained in confidence. It is important, however, not to lose sight of the fact that quite a proportion of the archives in the United Kingdom are still retained by their respective creators, whether institutions, families or individuals, and by no means all of these are available for research in the same way.

Even if there were a greater degree of central control it would not be easy to devise a monolithic public archive service that would satisfy every researcher's needs all the time. However you assemble archives – territorially, chronologically, thematically, by medium, or on grounds of national interest – you are bound to cut across the research interests and strategies of some categories of scholars. In practice, to accommodate all the surviving archives we need a combination of all these different approaches, and the very diversity of repositories is one of the strengths of the 'network'.

Standards

The age of infancy is over, both for our record offices and for the archive profession that has risen with them in the past half-century. We know exactly what we must do to preserve our archives in good shape, but it requires continuing commitment and resources on the part of the governing bodies that take on this responsibility – resources so considerable, in fact, and generally so hard to obtain on the regular basis that is required, that we must not allow them to be dissipated through the establishment of a multiplicity of small and poorly resourced repositories. If the job of preserving the written heritage is worth doing, it is worth doing well. And that surely should be a source of both national and local pride. It is something tangible we can do now to hand on a living awareness of the lives and achievements of our past citizens and communities. Would we not expect future generations to do the same for us?

Fortunately there is every evidence that, taking the United Kingdom as a whole, the job *is* being done well. Standards of care for our archives are continuously improving. A recent survey[20] showed that over 100 national, local authority or university archive buildings had been newly built, purpose-adapted or substantially refurbished between the first publication (1977) of British Standard 5454 *Recommendations for the storage and exhibition of archival documents* and the end of 1992. The rate of progress has continued, with new buildings or extensions since that date for, amongst others, the Public Record Office (Kew), the Scottish Record Office (Edinburgh), the National Library of Wales (Aberystwyth), the Royal Commission on the Historical Monuments of England (Swindon), the University of Warwick Modern Records Centre and BP Archives (Coventry), the county record offices of Greater London, Hampshire, Leicestershire and Shropshire, and

23   Thomas Thomson House, the new building of the Scottish Record Office

Westminster Archives Centre. Plans are currently on the drawing board for several more.

If we are to respect the archives we have inherited, and to hand them on in excellent condition to future generations, we must store them in a stable environment conforming to the British Standard; we must rigorously protect them against fire and theft; we must maintain them in good condition, which requires (i) a good-housekeeping or 'preservation' strategy, including perhaps the provision of surrogate copies of the material in most demand, in order to spare the originals from wear and tear, but also (ii) a conservation strategy for remedial work on damaged items; and we must arrange and describe them in accordance with accepted professional standards, and bring the resulting finding aids to wide notice, both locally and through the National Registers of Archives, and increasingly through computer networks.

The means of achieving this whole programme have to be considered before any new archive service is contemplated. Turning a blind eye to any of the individual elements could result in the loss, neglect or deterioration of the archives, or their costly and self-defeating accrual with little possibility of their being properly accessible for research.

In 1990 the Royal Commission on Historical Manuscripts published *A standard for record*

24 Westminster Archives Centre new building.

repositories, giving guidance to governing bodies on best practice with regard to the setting up and administration of record offices and archive services. It covered questions of constitution and finance, and policies on staffing, acquisition and access. In the same year the Museums and Galleries Commission, on behalf of a joint working party of the professional bodies of museum curators and archivists, first published its *Code of practice on archives for museums in the United Kingdom*.

The buck stops here

With a fully-fledged archive profession; increasingly numerous, articulate and organised user groups; a network of repositories extending across the whole country; and Standards as yardsticks against which we can measure whether we are storing and preserving archives in the best possible way, there is no excuse of the kind that might have been wheeled out say forty years ago for neglect or other half-measures. Those who formally undertake the care of archives enter into a kind of trusteeship, to ensure that our written heritage is handed down to future generations in at least as good a shape as when we accepted the challenge ourselves. The responsibility transcends today's fleeting 'ownership' or 'custody'. Archives are the building-blocks of everyone's history, the memory of our society as a whole and the means by which its leaders and its institutions can ultimately be held to account. Archives are a major part of our common heritage. Some would add that they are the very key to our continuing democracy.

The National Registers of Archives

The **National Register of Archives** maintained by the Royal Commission on Historical Manuscripts, and the **National Register of Archives (Scotland)** maintained by the Scottish Record Office, aim to discover the nature and whereabouts of all archives and records of historical importance, whether in public or private custody. They maintain lists of many of these archives for public consultation, as well as

information about their custodians and the terms and conditions of access. Remote access to the computerised indexes of the NRA is now possible through the Internet.[21]

The national, or 'public', record offices

The **Public Record Office** (1838), now based at Kew, is the principal repository for the archives of the United Kingdom's central government and associated bodies, and of the royal courts of justice.[22] They extend from Domesday Book (1086) to the present day and are a treasure store for historians of all periods, and indeed one could almost say of all countries. The PRO also holds important private archives, including many of those of the Duchy of Lancaster, papers confiscated by the state at various times in the past, documents submitted in evidence to courts of law and never reclaimed, and in particular certain papers of statesmen, politicians and diplomats, mostly in cases where the papers have a close affinity to the official records. Today, however, it does not normally take in private papers even of national interest. These are usually offered to or bought by the British Library or another appropriate national repository.

The PRO has no direct responsibility for records of state which had strayed from public custody before it was itself established or which, although of a public nature, have never been in public custody. As we have already seen, some of these have come to rest in private hands or in other public collections, for example at the British Library, the university libraries of Oxford or Cambridge, and Lambeth Palace Library. In a recent survey of the papers of 18th-century British diplomats, Jeremy Black identified relevant holdings not only in the PRO but also in the British Library, the Scottish Record Office, the PRO of Northern Ireland, the House of Lords Record Office, the National Maritime Museum, the National Libraries of Scotland and Wales, a score of local authority record offices, at least half a dozen university libraries, the Royal Archives and a number of private collections in the UK, not to mention foreign archives in Austria, Germany, the Netherlands, Sweden and Switzerland.[23]

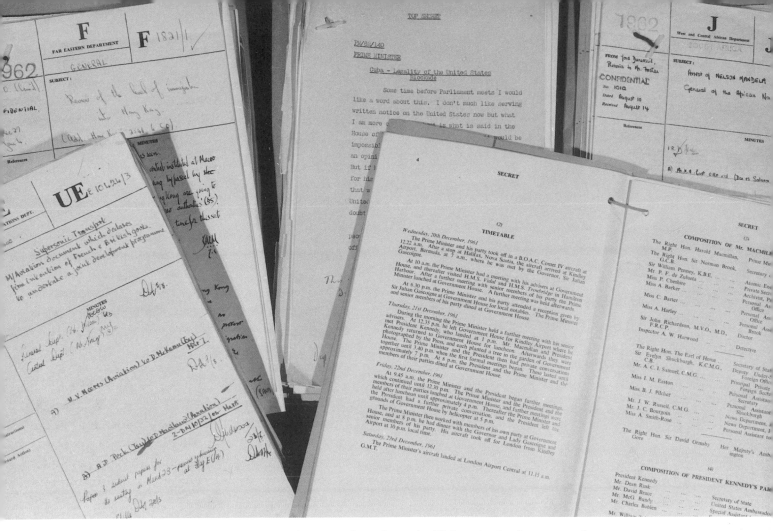

25   Preparing papers for press release day at the PRO under the thirty-year rule

In England and Wales, Public Records of strongly local interest – including Quarter Sessions, county court and coroners' records, hospital and pre-1858 probate records – even though they remain under the statutory charge of the Keeper of Public Records – are almost always deposited in other approved repositories around the country, many of them run by local authorities. Public Records kept on special media, and administrative records of some non-departmental public bodies and national museums etc, are also held in places of deposit appointed by the Keeper. In all, something like 25% of the Public Records are out-housed, in 250 places of deposit. The costs are borne locally. The PRO does not exercise any control over other aspects of local authority archive services, which are separately described below. Nor does its writ run over the records of Scotland and Northern Ireland. However, the convention is that similar rules are followed in all the national record offices of the UK for opening records to the public.

The **Scottish Record Office** in Edinburgh (so called in recent times, but founded as the General Register Office in 1787) is the national archives of Scotland, having responsibility not only for the records of Scottish departments of state and courts of law, but also (to a greater extent than in England) for records of local government and those of the Established Church. It also accepts gifts and deposits, and purchases private papers on a large scale. The Keeper of the Records of Scotland has more general oversight of archives than his English counterpart. This was reflected in the requirement of the Local Government (Scotland) Act 1994 that local authorities should consult the Keeper before setting up new archive services or making significant changes to existing ones. The Keeper also has the power to declare documents which were created by a public body to be *extra commercium*, and therefore recoverable if put up for sale.

Fog cleared up to day — still damp & very miry —
up 7 — at it continually until 11.30 then when I went to
FRIDAY, 12th FEBRUARY, 1886.
Port — the most busy day I've had there yet — office
(43·322)
full almost uninterruptedly from 11.30 until 4.40 —
sometimes 6 or 7 there at same — Two very good new matters —
one a bastardy case from Dyffryn — farmer's son — his father very
anxious I should appear — E.P. Owen recommend'd me — told father &
son that judging from the evidence they had very poor chance of succeed —
nevertheless he preferred I sh'd go there — p'd me £3.3.0 at once — feel
very elated over my success —

Pd £5 train to Blaenau to attend David's meet'g — my bro'r &
Edwin going with me — I went per invitation to Dr E's house —
Phil Thos James there — Dr wanted me to speak at meeting tonight. I told
him I was unprepared but he would have it — then I began to gnaw my
fingers that I had spent my time play'g drafts at café & fiddling with
Society boys instead of a prepar'd speech for such an occasion —
I feared I had thro' my own folly lost a grand opportunity —
I went to meeting having no intention whatever of spouting when
M.D. Jones announced at commencem't of meet'g that I was to speak there —
I was astounded — Hall packed — many keen men there in good position —
However after listening to Michael Davitt I retired to a room there —
a sort of lobby & amid the noise & bustle of speakers & spoken to & the talk
of some turbulent youth in the anteroom I tried to spin out a speech —
Got on very well — I had a few ideas upon the question so
I determined to set them together with a few extempore ideas — I hit upon
a good joke, I tho't, about Michael wrestling with the devil & one or
two other good hits — As my turn approach'd & I was getting late I
decided not to spout — when called on I had made up my mind
simply to apologize to them on the ground of the lateness of the hour &
fact of my not receiving notice — I tho't I w'd just try on the joke about
Michael — I did so & it created a roar of laughter — the audience began
to listen & beamed at me — thus encourag'd I went on amid
cordial & warm plaudits — my extempore hits taking best — one of
them evoking two rounds of cheering — I was now on my legs &
I spoke with great warmth & vigour both of gesture & voice — when
I sat down there was loud cheering & I felt that I had made my
mark at Festiniog & that was better there were present men from
all the surrounding districts from Form to Blaenau & thence
to Traws fynydd — I have made a good thing of a splendid
opportunity — Regarding Michael Davitt I am very
favourably impressed by his presence — he appears to be

The **Public Record Office of Northern Ireland** (1923) in Belfast is the single official repository in the province, although some local, university and specialist libraries have small archival holdings. Because of PRONI's all-embracing legislation it is, unlike the other public record offices in the UK, empowered to receive official records of every possible provenance. It holds records of government departments from the 19th century and of local government from the 18th century, as well as of the courts of law; and records and papers of private origin (mainly from the 17th century to the present, the earliest, however, being from the 13th century) emanating from individuals, families and estates, and institutions including businesses (a particular strength), the churches, hospitals and schools, trade unions and political parties.[24]

The National Libraries

There is no national record office in Wales, and the PRO currently serves both England and Wales. The **National Library of Wales** (1909) in Aberystwyth was established long before there were any local authority record offices there. Its holdings include the official records of the Court of Great Sessions (but not those of the county assizes, which are in the PRO), records of public bodies such as the Church in Wales and the Calvinistic Methodist Church, the Welsh Arts Council and Wales TUC; and many private archives of families and individuals, of manors and estates, and of business and industry.[25] In 1983 it established a **Welsh Political Archive**, 'in response to the realisation that many records and papers important to the political history of Wales had been lost forever'. Its holdings now include the archives of Plaid Cymru, the Labour Party in Wales, and the Welsh Liberal Party, including some local associations and branches.

The **British Library** in London, which sprang in 1973 from the British Museum (1753) and several other libraries of national importance, is the national library for the United Kingdom. As such it has accumulated substantial holdings of manuscripts and archives of all kinds, including many strayed state papers, as well as private papers of individuals prominent in every sphere of our national life. Since 1982 it has also administered the archives and manuscript collections of the former **India Office**, and since 1983 the **National Sound Archive**. In its *Annual Report* for 1992/93 the Library calculated that it held some 283,000 units (ie volumes or individual items) of manuscripts plus a further 260,000 from the India Office; as well as over a million sound disks and tapes, and 198,000 photographs.

The **National Library of Scotland** in Edinburgh (1927, but arising from the collections of the College of Advocates founded in the 1680s) is similarly rich in manuscript and archival holdings relating to Scotland, including legal papers, literary manuscripts, family muniments, the correspondence and papers of Scots prominent in many walks of life, and a number of important publishers' archives.

Other national repositories

Among other national repositories, the **House of Lords Record Office** holds the archives of Parliament and associated private papers. The **national museums and galleries** in each part of the United Kingdom, and similar nationally-funded bodies, often have departments of archives and manuscripts which, as well as the administrative records of the institution itself, hold and/or actively take in material within their specialist field of interest. The respective **Registrars General** of births, marriages and deaths in London, Edinburgh and Belfast retain their own records, whilst probate records since 1858 for England and Wales are retained by the **Principal Registry of the Family Division** in London.

Universities

The next major partners in the care of archives in the public sector are the universities and their constituent colleges.

Historical and geographical circumstances as well as deliberate academic strategy have helped

26   Page from Lloyd George's diary, 1886, at the National Library of Wales

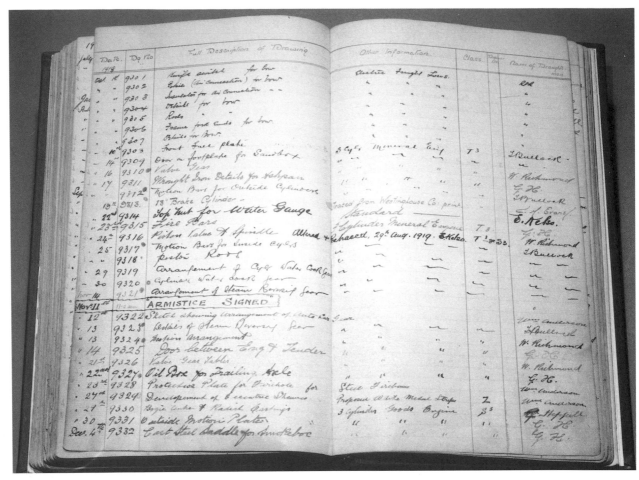

27 Drawing register from the Darlington Works of the North Eastern Railway 1918, now in the National Railway Museum, York. Note the incidental reference to the signing of the Armistice ending the First World War.

to determine the nature of their holdings. Where a university was in existence before any local authority record office in the area it sometimes took in private papers as a service to the local as well as the academic community. If so, it is still likely to have a continuing strength in local history, as at all the old-established Scottish universities, the University of Wales, Bangor, and (outside Oxford and Cambridge) the universities of Durham, Leeds, Manchester and Nottingham. In some cases universities took on pre-existing accumulations of archives as major research collections: at York, for example, diocesan and provincial records of the Church of England; at Durham the archives of the dean and chapter, including the medieval archives of the priory.

Elsewhere special collections have been built up to accommodate the papers of *alumni* and other friends and benefactors; to serve the research needs of particular departments or individuals; or to plug a perceived gap in the national provision for the protection of records of certain types, sometimes after a systematic survey.

Despite modest and sometimes financially shaky beginnings, many of these special collections have established themselves as of national and even international significance, serving a constituency well beyond their own academic and student body. Often, because of the wide-ranging careers and interests of the persons whose papers are held, the collections – whether or not they have a strongly thematic focus – will support wide interdisciplinary research. Here, for example, we find the main papers of many statesmen and politicians (Palmerston, Wellington, the Chamberlains, Churchill, Macmillan, Wilson); literary figures (Samuel Beckett, D.H. Lawrence); business archives like those of the shipping giant Cunard; and many manorial and estate records of our

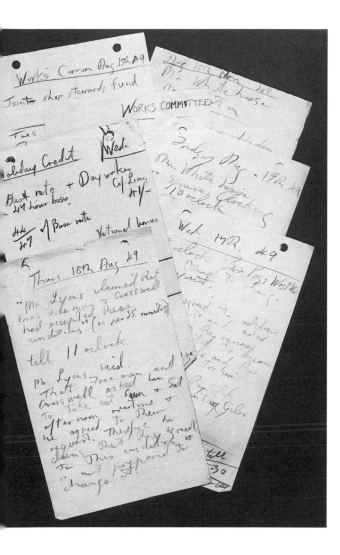

28 Daily working notes of Dick Etheridge, senior convenor at the Austin Motor Co., August 1949, now in the University of Warwick Modern Records Centre

29 The Revd C.G. Sparham of the London Missionary Society, at work probably in Hankow, China, where he was stationed from 1885 to 1917

ancient family or corporate estates. There are particular subject strengths, such as agriculture (Reading), business (Glasgow, Heriot-Watt), military history (King's College London), modern politics (Birmingham, Churchill Archive Centre Cambridge, British Library of Political and Economic Science at LSE, Bodleian Library at Oxford, Southampton), religion (Glasgow, Manchester, Leeds, Southampton, York), industrial relations and industrial politics (Warwick); the history of particular regions of the world outside the United Kingdom (Cambridge University Library, Durham University's Sudan Archive, London University's School of Oriental and African Studies, the Middle East Centre at St Antony's College Oxford, Rhodes House Library Oxford); particular chronological periods (Mass Observation Archive, Sussex), or particular media or forms of data (air photographs at Keele, ESRC data archive and

Qualidata Centre at Essex). The list could be greatly extended.

Together the universities now hold an estimated 125 shelf-kilometres of archives and manuscripts. Glasgow alone accounts for roughly a quarter of the total because of its formidable collection of business archives, as well as the university's administrative records and the library's special collections. At the other end of the scale are many colleges and universities with less than 100 metres of mainly administrative material. In between, the largest 20 university repositories each hold in excess of 1.5 kilometres of archives, although size is not always the most important indicator of the quality or historical importance of the material, and archives of national importance are to be found even among the smaller holdings.

Universities are playing a major rôle in surveying archival resources in specialist fields, whether or not they also seek to collect the records. To take just two examples, the National Cataloguing Unit for the Archives of Contemporary Scientists (Bath) offers a cataloguing service and practical advice on finding a home for archives, and Reading recently completed a survey of English literary manuscripts of the 19th and 20th centuries.[26]

Local authorities

The range and bulk of holdings of local authority archive services naturally vary considerably around the country. Their first duty is to the employing authority and its records, but a survey undertaken in 1992 showed that on average local authority records accounted for only 38% of holdings and Public Records another 11%. Just over half of all holdings, therefore, were of private origin, acquired by loan, gift or purchase. They include the official records and registers of the churches (particularly in England and Wales), papers of families and private individuals, of businesses and societies, and indeed of every conceivable kind of archive-generating body with a local connection, such as the following among the holdings of Birmingham City Archives: records of the Cherry Brandy Club, the

30 Accounts of collectors for the poor for the parish of St Margaret's Westminster, 14 Elizabeth I

Nondescripts Rambling Club and the Sutton Coldfield Poultry and Cage Bird Society.

Some of these archives are of intensely local significance; others have a wider (e.g. county, area or regional) context. Commonly in England and Wales, and to a lesser extent in Scotland, they are rich in material of interest to genealogists and family historians: church registers of baptisms, marriages and burials; manorial records; poor law records, and so on; and to these the record offices have often added microfilm copies of national material held elsewhere, such as the census returns or the International Genealogical Index of the Genealogical Society of Utah.

To an impressive extent local record offices hold records of importance for national or even international history. Papers of statesmen and politicians, of churchmen and industrialists, of important companies and organisations, and of many other individuals and institutions

mid-1970s and 1980s – many such records became casualties in the last two major restructurings of local government. Some were destroyed without adequate appraisal; many were abandoned *in situ* as premises were vacated; others were put into store and then quietly forgotten; the fate of quite a number more is still unknown. We are all the poorer for the losses to our archival heritage, and it may be salutary to remember that neglect and unthinking destruction are not entirely things of the distant past.

As if this were not bad enough, the law does not require local authorities to provide a more general archive service to cater for archives other than their own administrative and historic records. Fortunately, officers and elected representatives of local government have taken a broader view of their responsibility to protect and develop the local archival heritage.

England and Wales

The movement to take in historic records and papers, specifically so that they could be studied by the public, began with the great public libraries of the Victorian era in cities such as Birmingham, Bristol, Cardiff and Manchester. The first to appoint an archivist for this purpose was the City of London in 1876. Although county councils were established in 1889, and a number of counties thereafter established Records Committees to take stock of their archives, it was 1913 before the first county record office was established, in Bedfordshire. A dozen or so others followed before 1939, but the real growth has been in the past fifty years. In Wales the first was in Monmouthshire in 1938.

The loss or anticipated loss of archives during the Second World War reinforced the need for more initiatives of this kind and, in tandem with the development of the National Register of Archives, county council record offices began to spring up throughout England and Wales from the late 1940s onwards. The Local Government (Records) Act 1962 gave counties and the then county boroughs formal authority to acquire and care for private archives relating to their locality. As a result they consolidated their already substantial holdings of papers of private origin,

prominent in public life at a national level, are to be found in abundance in local custody.

The records of county government, from the origins of Quarter Sessions records in England and Wales in the 16th century, and of town and borough (burgh) administration throughout the UK from still earlier periods, rank among the most important sources for the history of our local communities. Some local authorities have taken particular pride in their official muniments, with the result that fine runs of archives have survived. Unfortunately this is not uniformly the case.

For practical reasons, as well as for their accountability to their electorate, local authorities throughout the United Kingdom nowadays have a legal responsibility to take good care of their own administrative records, both past and present. They are charged by the Local Government Acts to make 'proper arrangements' for this. This duty has been very variously interpreted and – to go back no further than the including family and estate papers and the records of many local businesses and institutions as well as certain statutorily controlled records such as manorial and tithe documents and the official registers and records of the Established Church, together with those of other churches, charities and societies.

This power was subsequently extended by ministerial Order to eight English cities. The London Government Act 1963 and the Local Government Act 1985 conferred the same powers on each of the London boroughs and metropolitan districts respectively, although by no means all of these have chosen to exercise their powers. In London a county-wide service, operating concurrently with the borough services (where such exist), is provided by the Greater London Record Office – run since 1986 by the Corporation of London. In the metropolitan counties a single county-wide service is provided in Tyne and Wear, a joint service in West Yorkshire, a county-wide service to complement that at district level in Greater Manchester, and district services in Merseyside, South Yorkshire and most of the West Midlands. By the time of the Local Government Act 1992 and Local Government (Wales) Act 1994, county record offices had been established in all the non-metropolitan counties of England and Wales except Avon, although figures published annually by the Chartered Institute of Public Finance and Accountancy show the authorities' widely varying expenditure on archive services, which bears no direct correlation to population or use but averages only about 50 pence per head of the population. Not surprisingly the standard of service is uneven.[27] At its best, however, it is outstanding. In the Parliamentary debate quoted at the beginning of this book, local authority archive services were variously described as 'a source of great local pride', 'cost-effective, well organised, widely respected', and 'vital if we are to protect the heritage'.

Scotland

In Scotland the pattern of development has been quite different. Up to the 1960s only three city-based services had been established, in Glasgow, Edinburgh and Dundee, and the Scottish Record Office provided substantial cover for the archives of the remainder of local government. The Local Government (Records) Act did not apply in Scotland, so there was less incentive than in England and Wales for local authorities to commit themselves to the work of caring for local archives on any wide scale. After the establishment of regional and island authorities in the 1970s a number of regional archive services were gradually set up, but of these only that serving the vast region of Strathclyde really resembled the scale of an English county record office. In Tayside, Fife and Lothian regions no regional service has been established. Services at district level are few. Many of the ancient burgh records were retained locally by the successor administrations or transmitted for safe keeping to the SRO. The Local Government (Scotland) Act 1994 gave Scottish local authorities powers similar to the Local Government (Records) Act 1962 for England and Wales.

The future of local authority archive services

From 1996, in England, Wales and Scotland, yet another new pattern of local government is to be implemented which will have far-reaching consequences for the delivery of archive services, and thus for the care of archives more widely.[28] Archive powers have been conferred on all the new unitary authorities established in England, Wales and Scotland. At the time of writing it is too early to be sure what effect this will have in practice on the provision of archive services.

It is clear that the government, in reforming the structure of local government, had no intention of weakening the archive network already in place. But the opportunity was missed, as it had been in 1972-74 and 1985-86, to introduce any mandatory element into the provision of an archive service by local authorities. The exact means by which the service would be delivered, in England at any rate, was left almost entirely to the local authorities themselves. Unlike the legislation for Scotland and Wales, the Local Government Act 1992 relating to England has no section specifically devoted to archives.

31 Grant to Tywardreath priory, Cornwall, of properties in Otterham parish, early 12th century

32 Travelling estate office

33 Private muniment room

Private archives and papers
Archives of families and individuals
Although private papers had already been given or loaned to public institutions such as the older universities and the great municipal libraries of the 19th century, the trend was substantially accelerated in the decades following the Second World War as more public repositories were established. Their custodians, together with the volunteers who helped at that time to develop the NRA, set about actively encouraging private owners to deposit their papers on loan, both for safe keeping and in order to promote public access.

Many owners needed little persuasion. In return for their public generosity in opening up their family or business archives, sometimes for the first time, they were spared the inconvenience and cost of keeping them at home, and there was the prospect of the papers being arranged, catalogued and if necessary repaired. On the other side of the partnership, these deposits helped to establish the reputation and credibility of the new repositories. They opened up research possibilities far beyond those that could be sustained by the governing body's own administrative records. True, the authority's archives and the private papers might complement one another, laying new foundations for the study of local and regional history. But the fact that so many of the private collections had wider significance, in proportion to the involvement of their creators, whether families or institutions, in regional and national affairs or in professional or business life, helped to lift the significance of the local (and where applicable the university) repositories on to a new plane.

In recent decades many of these individual archives have been sold by private treaty to the repositories which previously held them on loan, although regrettably others, or (often worse) parts of them, have been sold on the open market. The number of private collections of what might be called 'national' importance that have been sold has in fact risen steadily from two or three per year on average in the 1970s to seven or eight per year in the early 1990s, and although the grant-awarding bodies have been generous in their support, the governing bodies of the repositories have had to make very substantial financial commitments, increasingly backed up with direct (and hearteningly successful) appeals to the public, to secure such major collections as the Arundell of Wardour papers (Cornwall and Wiltshire Record Offices, 1991/92) or the Panshanger papers (Hertfordshire 1993/94).

Although there has been a gradual drift of once privately-owned papers into public custody at both national and local level, by gift or sale, many of the principal private collections of family, estate and business archives remain in private hands, whilst new ones are of course being accumulated with each succeeding generation. Some of the largest family archives retained in private hands are in the charge of professional archivists. These include, for example, the Royal Archives (Windsor Castle), the Duchy of Cornwall archives, and those of some of the older landed families. In the latter case a **Historic Houses Archivists' Group** provides a forum for the custodians. Other private owners, whilst retaining their archives, have come to an arrangement for their care, maintenance, and sometimes their study, with a nearby record office. However, in cases where there is neither an archivist nor any arrangement with the record office, researchers cannot safely assume that such archives will be readily available for study.

Private owners receive no public funding towards the upkeep of any papers retained at home. Some who genuinely want to encourage public access by *bona fide* scholars therefore have to make a charge to cover the costs of supervision. Unsupervised access is unwise, and access to completely unsorted and unlisted archives carries almost as great a risk. Security, staffing and cataloguing considerations of this kind, as well as the owners' need to preserve their own privacy or get on with their own work (which may well be conducted away from the place where the papers are stored) may make it quite impractical to allow public access.

The Historical Manuscripts Commission's guide to *Principal family and estate collections*[29] shows how some of the most important collections have taken shape, affected by descent

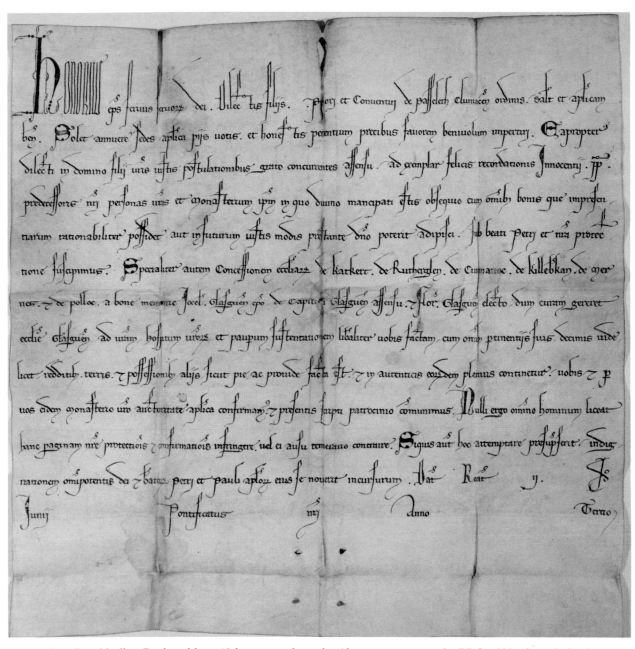

34 Papal bull to Paisley abbey, 13th century, from the Abercorn papers in the PRO of Northern Ireland

from one generation to the next, by marriages and family settlements, by the purchase and sale of lands, and so on. The wide geographical base of many of these families and estates means that papers of significance for the history of one area – not only matters directly connected with the land and estates but also industrial and business concerns, patronage of Parliamentary seats, presentations to church livings, and so on – will often be found in a private archive that is now housed in another county, possibly even at the opposite end of the country. The archives of the

Dukes of Portland, for example, accepted for the nation in lieu of tax in 1986, ranged far beyond the principal family seat at Welbeck in Nottinghamshire, and in fact right round the country from Cumbria to London, from Herefordshire to Northumberland, and into Scotland and Ireland.[30] To take another example, the oldest document currently held by the Public Record Office of Northern Ireland is actually of Scottish origin, one of a series of papal bulls granted to Paisley abbey in the early 13th century, to be found among the Abercorn papers.[31]

35 Magna Carta 1215, from the archives of the Dean and Chapter of Salisbury

Public repositories mostly continue to welcome private papers. A few, concerned at the occasional withdrawal of a loaned collection for sale on the open market, prefer whenever possible to negotiate the transfer to themselves of outright ownership, by gift or purchase. But there have been other changes in recent years in the relationship between owner and custodian. Pressure on storage space as repositories have struggled to keep up with the relentless pace of accessions, as well as pressure on staff and financial resources for cataloguing, conservation and public services, have led some custodians to advocate a more rigorous approach to accessions. To a greater extent than in the past, they now reserve the right to reject, or take only selections from, offered material in order to ensure that only material of lasting research potential is taken in. Commonly too, written loan agreements have been developed (at least for new loans). These spell out what owner and custodian have the right to expect of one another. They usually include provision, in the event of a future sale of the papers, for the first offer to be made to the repository itself in recognition of the time and skill spent in caring for them over the years.

Institutional archives

The archives of many societies, charities and institutions have also found their way into public repositories by gift or loan. Where these have a narrow and obvious geographical context they have often gravitated towards a local authority repository. But in the case of nationwide charities and voluntary organisations, considerations such as the field of activity of the organisation rather than the location of its head office might be a determining factor. In some fields a centre has been established to cater for the archives of similar bodies on a regional or national basis, as in the case of Scottish Jewish Archives and Scottish Catholic Archives. On the other hand, very many private institutions in fact retain their own archives, and some have developed into special repositories, taking in archives more widely within their particular sphere of interest. They include learned and professional bodies; national research institutes of all kinds; Royal Colleges, Societies

and Institutions in the scientific and medical fields; Lambeth Palace Library and a number of Anglican cathedral libraries; Roman Catholic diocesan archives and many other religious bodies such as monastic communities, theological colleges and missionary societies; some of the older schools; and antiquarian and archaeological societies. Further information on these and other custodians of archives can be found in the directory *British Archives*.[32]

Business archives

Some countries, like France, have taken so seriously the need to care for their business archives that they have established large national centres for this purpose. Something of the sort was the aspiration of English economic historians as long ago as the 1920s, but it has never proved

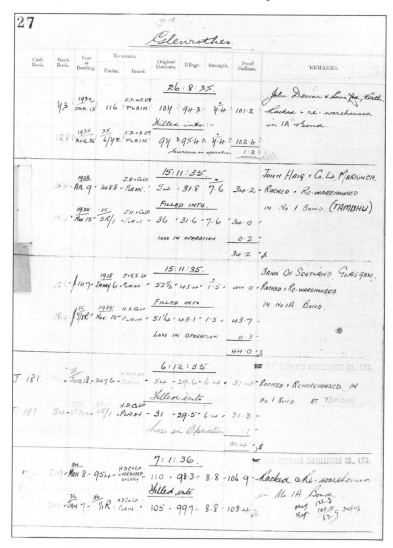

36   Racking book of Highland Distillers, 1935/6

47

37   Advertisement for the Wrexham Lager Beer Co. Ltd., *c.*1900

possible to raise the necessary funds, and it is arguably not the most convenient strategy for scholars, especially if the businesses in question have a strongly local context. The effort of rescuing, cataloguing and conserving business archives has therefore been quite widely dispersed, but because of the considerable bulk of production and administrative records associated with many businesses it can still occasionally be a problem to find repositories with the space and resources to accommodate them.

Many of the archives of business, industry and commerce have been taken in for safe keeping and public access by national, university and local record repositories. Some, like Glasgow University Archives Business Records Centre (with generous private sponsorship), have developed this as a special interest, wide-ranging in terms of both the locations and natures of the businesses covered. Many other university and local repositories have taken in the archives of particular firms or industries.

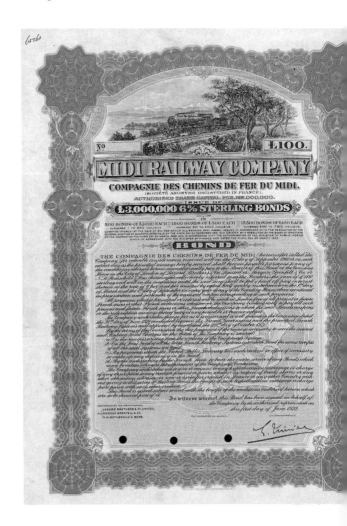

38   Railway bond of the Midi Railway Company, 1922
from the Rothschild Archives

Over and above these, it should not be forgotten that a great many family and estate papers also include material of direct relevance to business history. The recent guide to the department of Manuscripts and Records at the National Library of Wales, for example, draws attention to the importance of its holdings of private papers for a history of the iron, coal and copper industries in Wales.

A number of companies and businesses play a more direct rôle with regard to their own archives, appointing professional staff to provide

archives, and to avoid misunderstandings and disappointment intending researchers should always check in advance of any visit the terms and conditions on which access may be granted.

The archives of many businesses are of wider national and even international significance. Banks and other companies trading internationally, for instance, often have archives which shed important light on British relations with other countries. The sheer quantity of the records and correspondence can be daunting. The Rothschild Archive in London, for example,

39 The University of Warwick Library extension, housing the Modern Records Centre and BP Archive

archives and records management services, sometimes purely for their own in-house needs but increasingly with an eye to assisting the public as well, and sometimes offering educational services and outreach to the local community. A directory is published by the Business Archives Council,[33] which also keeps a weather-eye open for business archives which have fallen victim to the 'down-sizing' or collapse of the parent body, and offers advice on the future of their records. For commercial and other reasons, extended closure may apply to certain kinds of business

includes over 1˜ million letters to and from the partners and their agents throughout the world. But an archive of this size and distinction sheds light on many other historical issues: religion and society, charitable work and scientific innovation are among the areas cited in the Archive's current brochure. BP Archives recently entered into a unique arrangement with the University of Warwick's Modern Records Centre whereby the company and the Centre's archives occupy adjacent parts of a specially designed new building which has been jointly funded.

Two posters from the BP archives:

40 Poster attributed to 'Mansbridge' from the vintage year 1932.

41 Captain Eyston achieved this record breaking feat in his 21,236cc 12-cylinder Rolls-Royce aero-engined 'Speed of the Wind' in 1935

Not Just Paper with Writing

42 Coloured drawings by John Leighe, 1598, recording the glass then in All Saints' Church, Northampton

Archives are by no means confined to the formal written 'records' of central and local government, or for that matter of institutions or families. They include occasional printed matter, literary and musical works, sketches and drawings, maps and plans, photographs and (increasingly) films and sound recordings. Archive repositories have become both *de jure* and *de facto* custodians of all of these. That is not to say, however, that items falling into these various categories are in every case archival, and understandably the demarcation lines between archive repositories, libraries and museums are somewhat blurred in these areas.

Broadly speaking, published materials in any medium, as well as unique works of fine art intended primarily for display or sale, are not the concern of an archive repository. But they may be so if their separation from the wider archive of an individual, family or institution would seriously diminish its informational value. Moreover, as we shall see from a few examples below, even items which on this definition are *not* archival may for good reasons have been entrusted to the care of an archive repository.

Sometimes the archival association is absolutely clear-cut. Examples include:
- the master set of a charity's printed annual reports and accounts or of a parish's magazine, preserved alongside its administrative records;
- working drafts and the final (pre-publication) version of literary and musical works, preserved either among the originator's papers or in the archives of the publisher;
- architects' and engineers' drawings, whether among their firm's or their clients' archives;
- maps needed to administer an estate or utility;

- family and institutional photograph albums preserved among family papers;
- photographs and films officially commissioned by central and local government (or any other institutional creator of archives) for a purpose connected with their activities.

What many of these items have in common is that they might be prized on quite other than archival grounds, as works of art or things of beauty or scientific interest in their own right, and might therefore be collectors' items, liable to be detached from their archival context and treated as 'objects' on an individual basis, and of course the more vulnerable to sale as a result.

Literary and musical works

Drafts or completed texts of literary and musical works are frequently integral to the writer's own archive or to that of his/her publisher or patron, and so are potentially to be found wherever such archives have now come to rest. They may well, however, be more in demand for study because of the light they shed on the process of creating the finished work of art than for any historical or archival connotation. The wide cultural interest which they command even beyond our national boundaries makes them sought after either as complete archives or indeed as individual items if they come on the market in that form. They are thus particularly vulnerable to dispersal and export. North American universities and research centres have developed a special interest in the papers of modern British authors, whilst Japanese universities are particularly interested in the papers of British economic and political writers. Export controls apply to such papers only after they are fifty years old.

The national libraries maintain national collections of literary and musical works, including manuscripts as well as their published counterparts. There are important special collections too in a number of university libraries and departments, including some which perform a national function such as the Welsh Music Information Centre at University College Cardiff.

Many writers and composers have given or sold their original works to British institutions. The British Library, for example, recently received as a gift the working papers of the playwright Harold Pinter, CBE and purchased those of the composer Sir Peter Maxwell Davies. Acquisitions of older material are still pursued whenever possible. One of the treasures of the National Library of Scotland is Sir Walter Scott's 'Magnum Opus', purchased in 1985/86.

Around the country, a number of libraries, museums and research centres are dedicated to acquiring, studying and maintaining the archives and original works of designated writers and composers, among them the Britten-Pears Library at Aldeburgh (Suffolk), the Elgar Birthplace at Broadheath (Worcestershire), Brontë Parsonage Museum at Haworth (West Yorkshire), Keats House (Hampstead, London) and the Wordsworth Library at Dove Cottage (Cumbria).

Thanks to a recent survey undertaken at the University of Reading, we are now much the wiser as to the whereabouts of literary works written in English between the 18th century and the present.[34] No comprehensive survey of music collections has yet been undertaken. Specialist music collections are to be found not only in the national and university libraries but also in the music colleges and academies, and in centres such as Cecil Sharp House in London, the headquarters of the English Folk Dance and Song Society. But original scores are also to be found among the archives of individuals, families and institutions throughout the country. Two marches commissioned from Haydn during his second visit to England by Sir Henry Harpur for the use of the newly formed Derbyshire Volunteer Cavalry remained among Harpur's papers, eventually deposited on loan in Derbyshire Record Office. They were accepted for the nation in lieu of tax in 1994, to remain in the record office. The Malmesbury collection at Hampshire Record Office includes an air improvised by Handel and afterwards written down in his own hand.

A number of opera and ballet companies and orchestras maintain their own archives, whilst the archives of many amateur groups such as choral

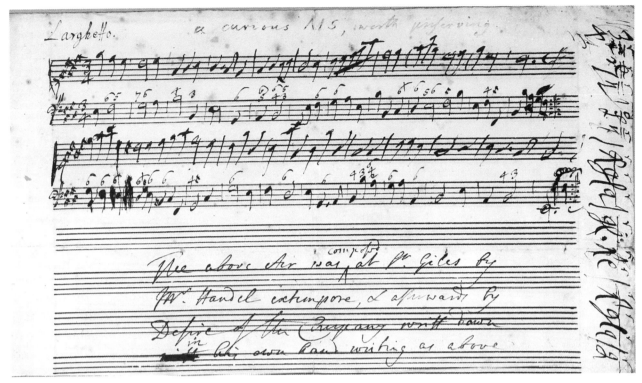

43   Handel autograph

societies and local bands have been deposited in local record offices. Special collections relating to drama have also been established, for example by the Theatre Museum in London and by the University of Bristol.

Maps

It is impossible to do justice to such a rich historical resource as maps and plans in a few paragraphs. Fortunately the need is diminished by the late Helen Wallis's *Historian's guide to early British maps* (1994)[35] which extends from the earliest surviving plan in the 12th century to the beginning of the present century. It might be pertinent to emphasise that apart from the national and local reference library collections, which almost always embrace (and in some cases may be limited to) commercially published material, there are very substantial map holdings in many archive repositories.

Indeed, many maps *are* archival, having been prepared to the order of (for example) the crown, central or local government, the armed forces, or the major corporations and estates, retained

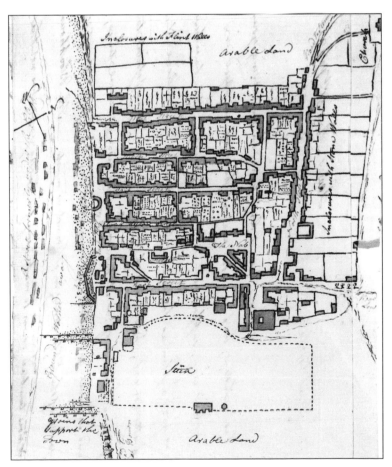

44   Plan of Brighton, 1773, drawn from memory by William Green of Lewes, showing areas washed away by the sea

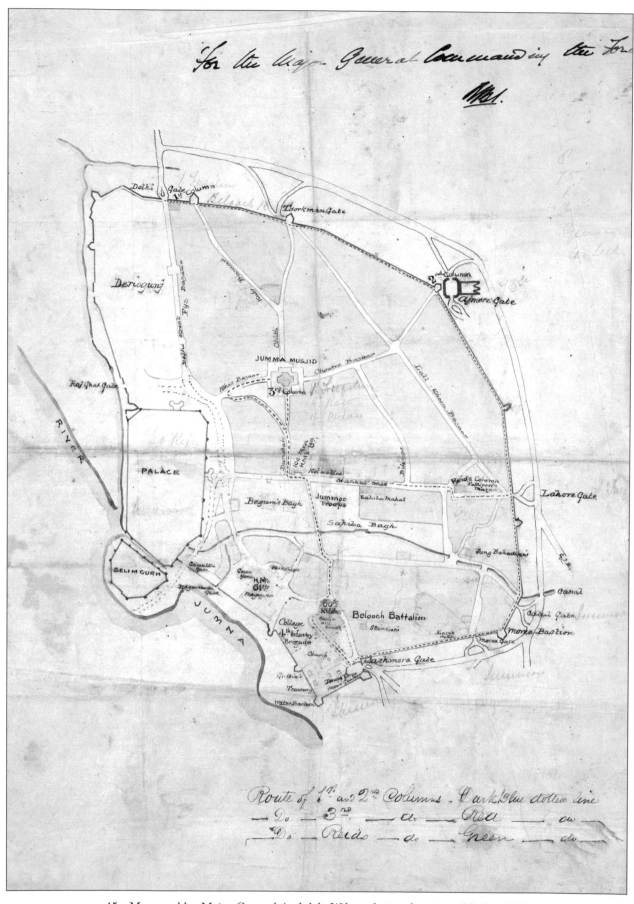

45   Map used by Major-General Archdale Wilson during the siege of Delhi, 1857

among their respective archives and often intimately connected to other documentation to be found there. It is not the distinction between manuscript and print that determines whether or not a map is archival, but rather the context in which it was created and used. For example, published maps which have been annotated in the course of use, such as Inland Revenue valuation maps, or which have otherwise been integral to a decision-making process, may very well themselves be a legitimate part of an archive. The archival context can quickly be lost if maps are seen as objects or works of art in their own right and hived off into a collection or, worse, sold off as separate items at auction. This is probably an unstoppable trend, although many of our archive repositories as well as the national libraries have raised the money necessary to purchase such items and in some cases reunite them with associated records or papers.

The three public record offices, in London, Edinburgh and Belfast, have substantial holdings of archival maps. In the case of the PRO they number something like six million, and their identification and cataloguing presents commensurate problems. These maps stem from every aspect of governmental activity, in Britain and overseas, and range from individual maps and plans produced to illustrate a point in a court of law to large series such as admiralty charts or tithe maps. The British Library and National Library of Scotland likewise have major map collections, and among many other national institutions mention should be made of the National Army Museum, the National Maritime Museum, the Admiralty Hydrographic Department and the respective Geological and Ordnance Surveys in Great Britain and Northern Ireland.

Archival maps are also strongly represented in local authority and university archive repositories. Typically they cover agriculture and land use including mining, enclosure and tithe; roads and navigation; military and naval campaigns; and (often by far the most numerous) planning consents; and frequently many other matters besides. Family and estate papers and the archives of estate agents and land surveyors, whether in public custody or not, can be rich in maps and plans, and some of the older-established corporate estates, like those of the established church in England (Church Commissioners, cathedral and diocesan archives), the Oxford and Cambridge colleges, the City of London livery companies, and the ancient schools and hospitals have their own estate maps. What is more, the wide extent of the great family and corporate estates tends to mean that maps which relate to one part of the country are quite commonly to be found in another.

Finally, mention should be made of the many learned bodies and research institutions that have special holdings of maps. They include, for example, the Royal Geographical Society, the Geological Society, and a number of archaeological societies.

Photographs

Photographs categorised primarily as works of art, or as examples of particular techniques and processes, quite naturally find themselves in museums and galleries for display or scientific study. Some institutions such as the National Museum of Photography, Film and Television in Bradford, the Fox Talbot Museum of Photography at Lacock and the Royal Photographic Society in Bath, have a specialist interest in photographs *per se*. The national libraries each have large collections, whilst many of the national museums and a number of university departments hold photographic collections illustrating their own fields of special interest, ranging from the vast military collections of the Imperial War Museum and the University of Keele Air Photo Library to the ethnological collections of the Royal Museum of Scotland or the Ulster Folk and Transport Museum. Among other national collections the respective National Buildings and Monuments Records for England, Wales and Scotland deserve special mention.

In addition, many local and university repositories also hold very substantial quantities of photographs including glass-plate negatives.

46 Buff Bill's circus, *c.*1910 from the Herbert Cooper collection, PRONI

47 The Forth rail bridge under construction, *c.*1887

They range from the odd photograph enclosed in a letter or official report to whole series of officially commissioned photographs on a particular theme, or the entire archives of photographers or photographic businesses, such as the collection of George Garland (1900-1978) at West Sussex Record Office, or that of George Washington Wilson at Aberdeen University Library. Some two million images are held by Birmingham City Library alone.

Many photographs are documents of great social importance, depicting (in a way which the written word cannot match) how our forbears looked, how they passed their time and amid what social or environmental conditions; how a particular street or town appeared at a given date, what a particular machine or mode of transport looked like, and so on. Some have been reproduced to illustrate previous points in this book. They are a rich educational resource, and of course prime targets both for exhibition and for publications of the *Barchester in old pictures* variety that have proved so popular all over the country.

> *Pictures often complement the information provided by documents. For example, one of our earliest photographs shows Toddington gamekeeper Norman Snoxell with a poacher in about 1854 (Ref: Z 50/126/54). The diary of John Thomas Brooks of Flitwick (Ref: LL 17/283) tells us that the photographer, the Toddington antiquarian William Cooper-Cooper, received his photographic apparatus from London on 25 May 1853, while the Toddington burial register (Ref: P 8/1/16) informs us that Norman Snoxell was buried on 30 June 1855, aged seventy-three. Thanks to the background information supplied by the documents we are able to learn more about the picture and to date it fairly accurately.*
>
> Bedfordshire Record Office Newsletter 32
> (December 1994)

Almost every household has its own album(s), and it has been estimated that in Britain we take more than a billion photographs every year,[36] but only a proportion of these will ever be offered to or accepted by a repository for permanent keeping along with the family, business or institutional archive that sets their context. Cataloguing and indexing photographs can present formidable challenges, especially if the date and context are unrecorded, and in such

cases there may be some doubt as to whether they are worth keeping at all; but many repositories have developed techniques for making the best of the information to be gleaned from their photographs.

Photographs require special storage in a controlled, dust- and light-free environment if they are to survive as long as possible, and their conservation is a specialist discipline. With the advent of the National Lottery there is a new national source of funding for their conservation.

Film and sound archives

Unlike any of the categories previously described, film and sound recordings require not only a special storage environment but also special equipment for viewing/ listening. The National Film Archive (part of the British Film Institute) and the National Sound Archive (part of the British Library) respectively take the lead in maintaining national collections, and they are the places of deposit for government records in film and sound respectively. There is also a steadily growing number of regional film archives. Despite their names, the functions of these bodies are as much

48   Sound and vision. The Charles Parker Archive at Birmingham City Archives

'library' as 'archive' oriented. Their holdings include commercial output as well as archival film and sound in a stricter sense, which may or may not be accompanied by the associated documentation that gives it an archival context. That documentation, because it requires different storage conditions and no special equipment for study, may well be preserved elsewhere as a matter of policy. For example, government films are maintained by the National Film Archive, but the related files of the film-producing units within government are held by the Public Record Office.

Some of the radio and television companies, and most particularly the BBC, maintain their own collections, which if they are intended for internal reference and re-use may be unavailable for public consultation. Others have entrusted their holdings to one of the existing national or regional film or sound archives, or indeed to a more general archive repository. Many of the latter now have small holdings of archival film and sound recordings (though not always adequate facilities to make them publicly available). Some, on the other hand, have developed a regional rôle for these media, as for example Hampshire Record Office for the Wessex Film and Sound Archive, and West Sussex Record Office in partnership with others for the South East Film and Video Archive.

A number of national museums, including the Imperial War Museum, the Royal Air Force Museum, and the Welsh Folk Museum, hold film and sound collections covering their respective fields of interest.

Film and sound recordings can be a major source of documentation in their own right, as in oral history projects, of which substantial collections have been made by many repositories and museums, often in connection with local history; or the Theatre Museum's video archive of live theatrical performances, or the British Library's National Life Stories Collection and Voices from the Holocaust. There may be debate about how far such productions are strictly 'archival', but they certainly cannot be ignored as a source of documentation and research material, and again as an important educational resource.

49

Electronic records

Relatively few computer-readable records have yet been transferred to archives, although the emergence from the 1960s onwards of data-sets that might merit further academic study led to the establishment of the Economic and Social Research Council's Data Archive covering the socio-economic and historical fields. In central and local government, the universities and business, the proper control and processing of electronic records has become an increasingly urgent aspect of modern records management and the national record offices issue guidance within their respective spheres.

Works of art and three-dimensional objects

Works of fine art, and three-dimensional objects whether hand- or machine-made or natural specimens, normally find a home in a museum or gallery or a special research centre rather than in a typical archive repository. They are likely to require special storage and handling, as well as special expertise for their interpretation. This is not to deny that in the right context they might be at least quasi-archival: for example in the case of geological or archaeological specimens held alongside the written reports that explain them, or samples and pattern books among the archives of manufacturing firms.

For local administrative or logistical reasons, or simply because they have acquired other related items, a number of archive repositories have nevertheless been entrusted with objects in these categories which are administered alongside the rest of the archives. West Sussex Record Office, for example, holds a major collection of engravings, drawings and printed works by Eric Gill, and received a small grant from the National Manuscripts Conservation Trust towards its care in 1992. The Bardsley-Powell family and estate archive held by West Yorkshire Archive Service includes glass lenses of the astronomer and mathematician Abraham Sharp (1651-1742) which were subjected to X-ray fluorescence analysis by the British Museum in 1994.[37]

50   Fairground art from the archive of Ernest Barrett of Derby (d.1948)

A wide range of other artistic output has to be recognised as essentially archival, provided again that its archival context has been preserved. Take for example the drawings made by antiquarians of monuments or buildings they studied, like those of John Leighe illustrated at the beginning of this section; illustrated travel journals created by individuals and kept among their papers; official registers of patented designs; textile pattern books (which often include samples); master sets of posters whether of an informational or propagandist nature; illustrated estate surveys and proposals for landscaping, such as Humphry Repton's Red Books; or architectural drawings for country houses.

Finally, it is important not to forget all those truly archival documents which are also works of art in their own right, triumphs of penmanship, often exhibiting great self-confidence as well as a pride in the accurate maintenance of the written record. The illustration on the cover of this book is a good example.

51 A page from a Royal Doulton character jug pattern book

Protecting the Written Heritage

The essential first line of defence for our written heritage is a strong and comprehensive network of repositories which are able to provide rescue services, care and protection and controlled access to archives, and to information about archives, both public and private. We are well on the way to achieving this. But the network at present lacks a solid statutory framework; it is distinctly patchy in places, and it has a few obvious gaps. This is largely because its fortunes have depended, and continue to depend heavily, on the financial situation of generally hard-pressed institutions, especially in the public sector. Nevertheless, when we consider how much has been achieved by this incremental and substantially voluntary partnership over the past fifty years it is surely unthinkable to let the process slide into reverse, whether through under-funding or the kind of structural change now affecting local government and the universities. Archives have established themselves as a necessity in ours as in every other civilised society. Archive services have no less clearly become a valued academic and social amenity for all our citizens, and on an equal basis.

Conservation

Taking in the archives is not enough. By doing this the custodian enters into a moral contract on behalf of the rest of us, to look after them in perpetuity. The fulfilment of this obligation depends first on providing storage and research accommodation which meets currently accepted standards and minimises all risks, and secondly on more active intervention when necessary to protect and/or repair damaged or deteriorating items.

Virtually all the materials on which archival records are carried are subject to bio-deterioration and decay. These processes can be accelerated by exposure to inappropriate or unstable storage conditions, to the ravages of heat and damp, light, atmospheric pollution, mould and insect infestation, as well as the more obvious

52   Leicestershire Record Office's conservation studio

threats of fire, flood or theft, or wear and tear through excessive handling.

Researchers understandably prefer whenever possible to consult original documents, but the scale of damage through handling is now so great that many repositories have embarked on programmes to produce surrogate copies for study, usually in microform, to save the originals. For many purposes access to the information in this format may be sufficient. But more importantly, this may be the only cost-effective way to save the information in whole series of records quickly from irremediable decay.

Conservation has always been taken seriously by British archive repositories. Not only the large national organisations but also the great majority of county record offices in England and Wales have their own in-house conservation workshops. Where this is not the case, as in most of the London boroughs, many of the metropolitan districts, most Scottish local repositories and quite commonly among university libraries, standing arrangements are usually in place with another nearby repository or with conservators in the private sector.

In recent years custodians have developed wide-ranging 'preservation' strategies, to improve the conditions in which archives are stored, monitor their well-being, and identify those in most urgent need of attention. Some have calculated that to put every individual item from their holdings into pristine condition would occupy hundreds of staff-years, and a survey in the mid-1980s found that an estimated 20 shelf-miles of archives in our public repositories (out of a total of some 750 miles) were too fragile to handle. But fortunately they are not all equally in demand and the work can usually be prioritised.

Conservation problems on a massive scale are also experienced by libraries, the essential difference being that much of the material there exists in multiple copies and could (at a cost) be replaced if necessary, whereas archives are unique. The British Library makes grants to assist cataloguing and conservation in other libraries, a service which it has generously extended to record offices. When pressure on funds led the

53   Damaged archives undergoing humidification

Library to withdraw these grants for a time in the 1980s, the Historical Manuscripts Commission and the British Library jointly, with government and major private sector support, established in 1990 the **National Manuscripts Conservation Trust**, to give financial assistance to owners and custodians of manuscripts and archives judged to be of national importance. The Trust has launched an appeal to maintain this work, and donations are welcome; its address is included in the Appendix.

The Trust's grants of over £550,000 in its first five years have demonstrated yet again how much of our national written heritage is actually to be found outside the nationally-funded collections (which, for the most part, are ineligible for its support). Beneficiaries have included local authority record offices, libraries and museums; university libraries and museums; learned bodies and professional institutions; cathedral and college libraries and independent museums, as well as a small number of private owners whose papers are inalienable. The manuscripts treated have included papers of Jeremy Bentham, Charles Booth, Benjamin Disraeli, Samuel Johnson and the first Duke of Wellington; manorial and estate papers such as the muniments of the earldom of Berkeley and the Wakefield court rolls; papers of scientists and engineers, businessmen and entrepreneurs, travellers and explorers, artists and writers; medieval literary and illuminated manuscripts from as early as the 10th century; the records of ancient boroughs and gilds; architectural plans and topographical drawings; a host of ecclesiastical records including parish, diocesan and provincial archives of the established church in England; and a number of business archives including those of John Broadwood and Sons, piano manufacturers, Cammell Laird (Shipbuilders) Ltd and the Festiniog Railway Company.

The Scottish Record Office makes grants towards the conservation of archives in Scottish repositories. The National Heritage Memorial Fund (*see below*) has also occasionally supported archive conservation, most notably through grants to the British Film Institute for the restoration of early films in the National Film Archive.

Disposal of private archives

Private owners anywhere in the United Kingdom who for whatever reason can no longer retain their archives can obtain free advice from the **Royal Commission on Historical Manuscripts**, which for example can put them in touch with an appropriate repository to discuss the gift, loan, or perhaps sale of the archive. Owners in this position will usually better serve the interests of scholarship and the nation's 'memory' at large if they keep their archive together as a unity. Many important archives have suffered by the piecemeal sale of individual documents or by more general fragmentation at auction, where it sometimes happens that prices fail to reach expectations, and the integrity of an archive is damaged by the sale of a bit here and a bit there, and with little gain to the vendor. The papers of Earl Macartney (1737-1806), the diplomat, have been so widely dispersed by sale and descent that they are now to be found scattered in at least seven British repositories, one in the Irish Republic, a dozen in the USA, and others in India, Japan and South Africa.[38]

Successive governments, recognising a degree of national interest in privately owned archives, have introduced measures to encourage their transfer to public institutions. These include: fiscal measures such as the possibility of acceptance in lieu of inheritance tax, and the exemption from capital taxation of archives sold by private treaty to a public repository; grant-aid from public funds to assist repositories in the acquisition, conservation, storing and cataloguing of archives; and export controls.

Acceptance in lieu of tax

Since 1975, manuscripts and archives have been eligible for acceptance by the nation in lieu of inheritance tax. To qualify they must be of pre-eminent national, scientific, historic or artistic interest, but no minimum value is prescribed so they do not necessarily have to be either very highly priced or very extensive. The scheme has enabled the nation to acquire a number of great family and estate archives such as those of the Dukes of Newcastle (1981) and Portland (1986); the papers of statesmen and military figures (Blenheim papers 1977, Admiral of the Fleet Lord Fisher 1978, Wellington papers 1979), of musicians, artists and writers (Benjamin Britten 1979, Henry Williamson 1980, Sir William MacTaggart 1983, Sir Arthur Bryant 1986, Lord Clark 1987, Haydn marches from the Harpur Crewe papers 1994), and of scientists (George Constantinesco 1983, George Bellas Greenough 1991), as well as a number of important illuminated manuscripts.

Recipients of archives and manuscripts accepted in lieu of tax, 1976-1994

National libraries
British Library, National Library of Scotland, National Library of Wales

National museums and galleries
Imperial War Museum, Science Museum, Tate Gallery

University libraries and archive centres
Cambridge (University Library, and Churchill Archive Centre), Exeter, Leeds, London (University College), Nottingham, Oxford (Bodleian Library), Southampton

Local authorities
Bedfordshire, Hampshire, Nottinghamshire, Wolverhampton

Specialist repositories
Wordsworth Library (Dove Cottage)

Other
The National Trust

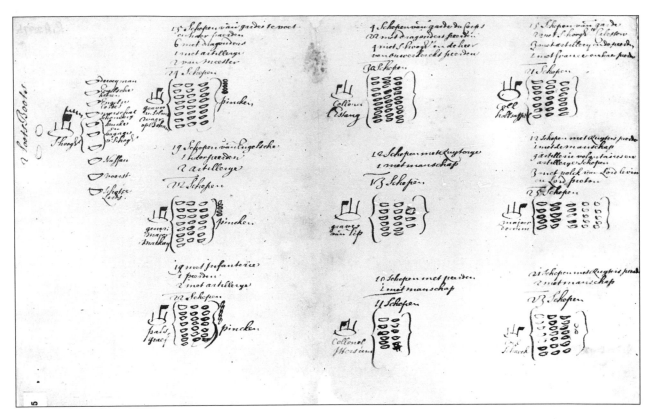

54 The Portland Papers accepted for the nation in lieu of tax and allocated to Nottingham University include this order of sailing of the Dutch fleet that brought William of Orange to England in 1688

Even items of lesser preeminence may be conditionally exempted from tax provided that the owner undertakes to make them available for study and not to dispose of them.

Private treaty sales

The state also subsidises a scheme whereby a vendor offering manuscripts for sale by private treaty to a public institution may be eligible to benefit from concessions on any capital tax liability attaching to the transaction, whilst the purchasing institution instead of the Inland Revenue may receive a sum equivalent to the balance of the tax due, in effect as a discount on the gross asking price. There are signs, however, that these arrangements are less effective in protecting the heritage than they once were. Tax thresholds have risen, and prices have to exceed a rising threshold before tax concessions become applicable. Legitimate tax-avoidance measures and off-setting of capital losses are reducing vendors' liability to capital taxation. Some private collections are vested in charitable trusts which have no capital tax liability. It is therefore by no means unknown for archives valued even at over £1 million to incur no capital tax liability on sale, with the result that no concessionary price can be negotiated.

Whether or not tax concessions apply, the government has also sought to underpin the efforts of public repositories to acquire archives, through the National Heritage Memorial Fund and a number of purchase grant funds.

The National Heritage Memorial Fund

In the period up to 1993/94, the National Heritage Memorial Fund (NHMF, established with government funding in 1980) had given 144 grants totalling almost £12.5 million (9% of its grant aid) to the purchase and conservation of manuscripts and archives, including such categories as architects' drawings, photographs and film. The average grant was £86,479.[39] But major collections of personal and family papers, as well as individual manuscripts of great artistic and literary significance, can now occasionally command what had previously been thought stratospheric prices applicable only to major works of art. An important threshold was crossed in 1989/90 when, for the first time, a grant exceeding £1 million pounds was paid, towards the purchase by the British Library of the Trumbull papers, a large archive including vitally important diplomatic correspondence for the early decades of the 17th century. In the very next year, however, the fund contributed a grant of over £2 million towards the rescue and rehousing of Hereford cathedral's medieval world map (Mappa Mundi). In its lifetime the Fund has contributed grants to national, local authority, university and special repositories (including for example Lambeth Palace Library), in all the constituent countries of the United Kingdom. It has helped save for the nation many wide-ranging family archives embracing the papers of statesmen, politicians and literary figures from the 16th to the 20th centuries and including almost forgotten original treasures such as Charles II's Secret Treaty of Dover and its attendant state papers, bought by the British Library from a private owner in 1987/88. Also strongly represented have been manuscripts and archives of literary figures (Jane Austen, William Cowper, John Evelyn, D.H. Lawrence, Hugh MacDiarmid, Sir Walter Scott, Evelyn Waugh), artists and architects (Augustus John, Charles

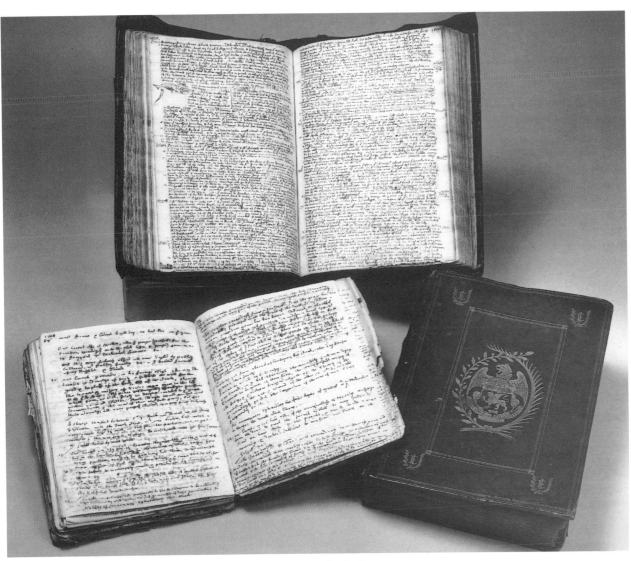

55 John Evelyn's diary

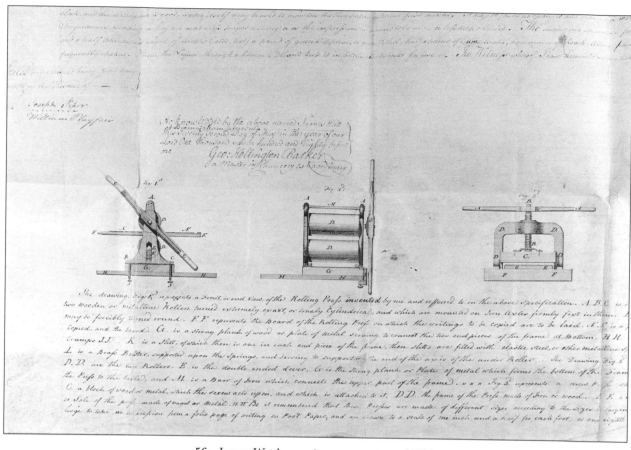

56 James Watt's copying press patent of 1780

Rennie Mackintosh, Walter Newall), military and naval figures (Lord Nelson, General Gordon), politicians from Walpole to Lloyd George, engineers (Isambard Kingdom Brunel, James Watt); and a number of prestigious individual manuscripts (the Rutland Psalter and the Murthly Hours, original scores of Haydn's London symphony and Mendelssohn's *Elijah*).

The NHMF now also administers the **Heritage Lottery Fund**, set up at the beginning of 1995 to administer the 'heritage' share of the proceeds from the National Lottery. This is able to make grants towards, among other things, the purchase, conservation, cataloguing and proper housing of archives and manuscripts. Among its first grants announced in April 1995 was the purchase, after complex and much publicised negotiations, of the papers of Sir Winston Churchill at a total cost of £12.5 million, to enable the papers to remain intact where they had long been on loan, at Churchill Archives Centre, Cambridge.

The purchase grant funds

Public money also supports three purchase grant funds, run respectively by the Victoria & Albert Museum, the Science Museum, and the National Museums of Scotland. In each case their original intention was to assist local museums in purchasing objects which might otherwise be lost to the nation, but all now include manuscripts and archives (and therefore record repositories) in their terms of reference. Concern that the items most vulnerable to loss and dispersal were manuscripts and archives of modest price in saleroom terms, but still beyond the normal means of record offices, led the V&A in 1973 to establish alongside its main fund a Manuscripts fund, which in its first twenty years of existence gave grants totalling over £800,000. For the more highly priced collections, however, access to the main V&A fund has always been a boon to archive custodians, and in the same period grants from this fund for archives have far exceeded

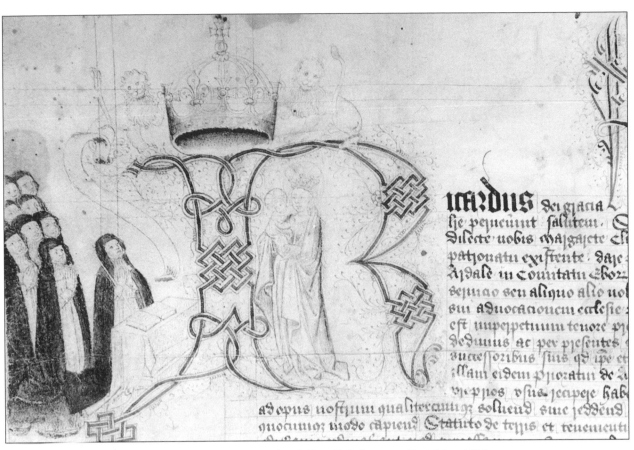

57   Letters patent of Richard III to Esholt priory, Yorkshire, 1485

£1 million. From the Science Museum (PRISM) fund and the Scottish fund, grants towards archives have been fewer and on a more modest scale, but a number of significant purchases have resulted, including for example the papers of Robert Fitzroy, captain of the *Beagle* at the time of Darwin's voyage, and the natural history drawings of Jonathan Couch of Polperro (Cornwall).

Export controls

If it comes to a question of export, archives and manuscripts over 50 years old, other than the personal papers of the applicant, require an export licence from the Department of National Heritage before they can legally leave the United Kingdom either permanently or temporarily. This applies irrespective of their monetary value, and irrespective of whether their destination is a country within the European Union or outside

it. Since there is no control on the export of manuscripts under 50 years old, and of the personal papers of living individuals, there have been some major losses of modern papers, particularly of modern literary manuscripts.

So far as material over fifty years old is concerned, the periodic reports to the Crown by the Royal Commission on Historical Manuscripts have shown that, since this system of export controls was put in place, there have been very few cases of the export of either substantial archives or individual items of outstanding heritage significance. Nonetheless, prodigious quantities of documents of lesser significance have indeed been exported. The loss is mitigated only by the British Library's selective retention of photocopies, on which however the exporter has the right (nowadays almost always waived) to impose a seven-year embargo on public access. The situation is kept under review by a Documents Working Party of the **Reviewing Committee on the Export of Works of Art**.

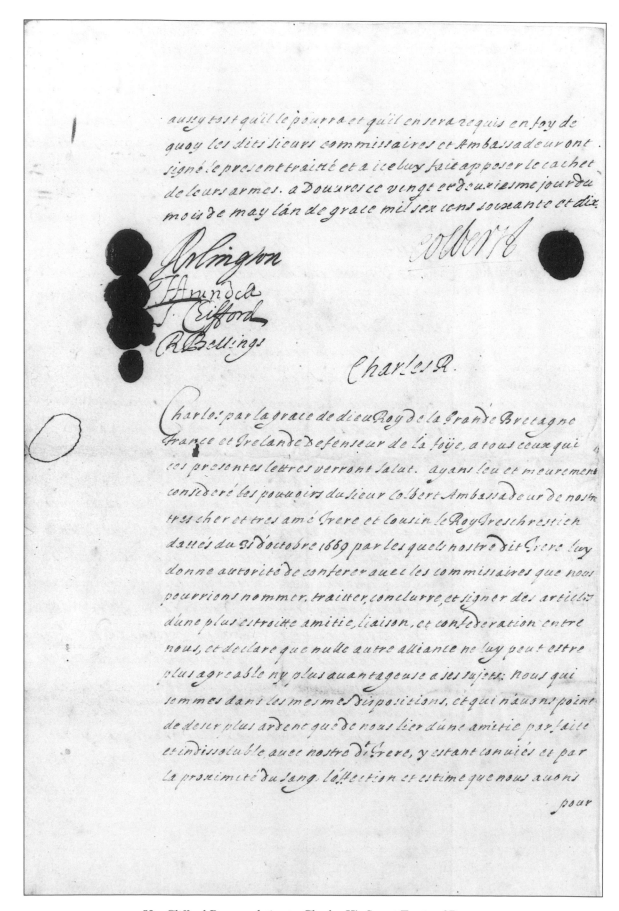

aussy tost quil le pourra et quil en sera requis en foy de
quoy les dits sieurs commissaires et Ambassadeur ont
signé le present traité et a iceluy fait apposer le cachet
de leurs armes. a Douvres ce vingt et deuxiesme jour du
mois de may lan de grace mil sex cens soixante et dix.

Arlington

Colberte

Harunda

T. Clifford

R. Bellings

Charles R.

Charles par la grace de dieu Roy de la Grande Bretagne
France et Irelande Defenseur de la foye, a tous ceux qui
ces presentes lettres verront Salut. ayans leu et meurement
consideré les pouvoirs du sieur Colbert Ambassadeur de nostre
tres cher et tres amé Frere et cousin le Roy treschrestien
datés du 31 d'octobre 1669 par lesquels nostre dit Frere luy
donne autorité de conferer avec les commissaires que nous
pourrions nommer. traitter, conclurre, et signer des articles
dune plus estroitte amitie, liaison, et confederation entre
nous, et declare que nulle autre alliance ne luy peut estre
plus agreable ny plus avantageuse a ses sujets: Nous qui
sommes dans les mesmes dispositions, et qui n'ausns point
de deser plus ardent que de nous lier dune amitie particulle
et indissoluble, avec nostre dit Frere, y estant convies et par
la proximité du sang, laffection et estime que nous avons

pour

58 Clifford Papers relating to Charles II's Secret Treaty of Dover

When an objection to export is lodged the case is heard by the Committee. If it upholds the objection a period is set in which a British institution has the chance to pre-empt export by paying the would-be exporter the full price of the document(s). If the money is found the exporter must either sell to the British institution or keep the document(s) in the UK. In its first forty years, up to 1992/93, the Committee heard 77 cases concerning manuscripts and archives. 36 resulted in the retention of the manuscripts in the United Kingdom; in a further two cases the request for a licence was withdrawn, and in one, the exporter being unwilling to sell to a British buyer, the item was placed under an indefinite export stop. About half of the cases thus resulted in retention of the manuscripts in the UK. In 13 cases, despite a temporary stop, no British institution came forward with an offer and export was allowed. In all but three of these the destination of the manuscripts was the USA.

Losses included illuminated manuscripts such as the 13th-century Northumberland bestiary (priced at over £3 million) and the 15th-century Clarence Hours; a 13th-century reissue of Magna Carta; a mock charter of Queen Elizabeth I to her Secretary of State Cecil; personal papers of two British explorers, James Bruce (1730-1794) and HM Stanley (1841-1904); and an album of early experimental photographs collected by the Revd Calvert Jones between 1839 and 1844. In a further 24 cases the objection to export was overruled. The great majority of these were of mainly literary or art-historical significance including illuminated liturgical manuscripts and photographs, but the list includes also a New Year gift roll of Elizabeth I, an 11th-century charter of Selby abbey, and the business archive of John Lane, publishers.

Papers saved for British institutions have included the Secret Treaty of Dover already mentioned; the company archives of Gillow's

59 Henry Purcell autograph

furniture manufacturers, and ledgers of Fribourg and Treyer, snuff manufacturers and tobacconists (both for Westminster City Archives), charters of the Augustinian priory of St Thomas the Martyr, Stafford (Staffordshire Record Office) and papers of the philosopher G.E. Moore (Cambridge University Library). Perhaps the most outstanding recent success has been the retention of a notebook containing the only keyboard compositions by Henry Purcell (1651-1695) known to have survived in his own hand (British Library). This was the first music manuscript ever to have been the subject of an export stop.

These examples, chosen from many others, illustrate not only the nature of the threat but also, once again, the rôle of every kind of public repository in preserving our national written heritage. At issue may be a single document or a large business archive, something priced at a few hundred or several million pounds, of any date up to the early 20th century, of historical, scientific, artistic or literary interest.

Conclusion

There are few grounds for complacency. The defences we have in place for the written heritage still leave a lot to chance. Perhaps the key to ensuring that they become and remain more effective is the widest possible dissemination of an awareness of the importance of archives to us all.

Readers who may be inspired to support our archives and archive services more actively could, for example, join one of the many existing Friends organisations associated with particular record offices (or help to establish one where none yet exists). There are also national organisations whose membership is open to all, including some of the constituent bodies of the National Council on Archives itself. They include, for example, the **British Records Association**, the **Scottish Records Association**, the **Historical Association**, and the **British Association for Local History**. The many family history societies around the country are represented by the **Federation of Family History Societies**, whilst the **Royal Historical Society** represents academic interests. Contact addresses for these and other bodies are given in the Appendix.

Notes

1. For these and other references to the Parliamentary debates throughout this section, see *Parliamentary Debates, House of Lords*, 17 Jan, 10 Feb, 7 & 30 Mar, 14 July 1994; *House of Commons*, 22 Mar, 24 May 1994.

2. See, for example, D. Keene and V. Harding, *A survey of documentary sources for property holding in London before the Great Fire* (London Record Society, xxii, 1985). 'A geographer navigates the Pipe Rolls', in *Hampshire Archives Trust Newsletter*, Spring 1995, p.28.

3. Royal Commission on Historical Manuscripts, *Annual review 1993-1994*, p.2. West Glamorgan: Annual report of the county archivist 1994-1995.

4. R. Hutton, *The rise and fall of Merry England. The ritual year 1400-1700* (Oxford, 1994).

5. N.A.M. Rodger, *The insatiable earl* (1993).

6. Hugh the Chanter, *History of the Church of York 1066-1127* (ed. C. Johnson, revised M. Brett, C.N.L. Brooke and M. Winterbottom, Oxford, 1990), p.3. 'Time and chance: the survival of records', in *Bedfordshire Record Office Newsletter* 20 (December 1991). A. Tough, 'Trade unions and their records', in *Archives* xix, no 83 (April 1990), p.121. Neil Ascherson, writing in *The Independent*, 17 July 1994.

7. J. Fuggles, 'The Kingston Lacy leaf', in *National Trust Magazine*, Spring 1993. York: *ex inf.* C.C. Webb, Borthwick Institute. *Bedfordshire Record Office Newsletter* 20 (Dec. 1991), p.2.

8. House of Lords, 10 Feb 1994.

9. D. Lay and C. Turner, 'Educational use of the Bass archive', in *Business Archives* 65 (May 1993).

10. House of Lords, 14 July 1994.

11. Suffolk Records Society, xxi (1980).

12. For further details see J. Maitland Thomson, *The Public Records of Scotland* (Glasgow, 1922); D. Stevenson, 'The English and the Public Records of Scotland 1650-1660', *Stair Society Miscellany I* (Edinburgh 1971), pp.156-168.

13. Cited by Gwyn Jenkins in 'Archives in Wales. The past in the future' (A lecture to the Honourable Society of Cymmrodorion, December 1994).

14. G.R.C. Davis, *Medieval cartularies of Great Britain: a short catalogue* (1958).

15. J. James, 'A lucky escape for Lymington', in *Hampshire Archives Trust Newsletter*, Spring 1995, p.36.

16. R. Hutton, 'Two newly-discovered Stuart State Papers', in *Archives* xx, no.90 (Oct 1993), pp.210-212.

17. Peter Payne, introducing L. Richmond and B. Stockford, *Company Archives* (1986).

18. A. Thick, ' "An experience not to be missed". The salvage of an archive', in *Journal of the Society of Archivists* xv, no. 2 (Autumn 1994), p. 175.

19. For further details see A.A.H. Knightbridge, 'Archive legislation in the United Kingdom' (Society of Archivists Information Leaflet 3, 1985).

20. C. Kitching, *Archive buildings in the United Kingdom 1977-1992* (HMSO, 1993).

21. (Internet address http://www.hmc.gov.uk). For further information see Dick Sargent (ed.), *The National Register of Archives: an international perspective. Essays in celebration of the fiftieth anniversary of the NRA* (*Historical Research*, Special Supplement 13, June 1995). This includes an article by Ishbel Barnes on NRA (Scotland). See also R.J. Olney, *Manuscript sources for British history. Their nature, location and use* (Institute of Historical Research Guides no 3, 1995).

22. For further details see the PRO's *Current Guide*. G.H. Martin and P. Spufford, *The records of the nation: the Public Record Office 1838-1988; the British Record Society 1888-1988* (Woodbridge, 1990). J. Cox, *The nation's memory. A pictorial guide to the Public Record Office* (HMSO, 1988).

23. J. Black, 'The papers of British diplomats 1689-1793' in *Archives* xx, no.88 (Oct 1992), pp. 225-253.

24. *Guide to the Public Record Office of Northern Ireland* (1991).

25. *Guide to the Department of Manuscripts and Records* (Aberystwyth, 1994).

26. For further reading see *The role and resources of university repositories* (Society of Archivists and SCONUL, 1989); B. Dyson, 'University repositories in the 1990s and beyond,' in *Archives* xx, no 88 (Oct.1992); M. Moss, 'Changes in the structure and financing of universities: the impact on archives and research collections,' in *Journal of the Society of Archivists* 13, no. 2 (Autumn 1992); *Surveys of historical manuscripts in the United Kingdom* (Royal Commission on Historical Manuscripts, 2nd edn, HMSO, 1994).

27. For further reading see H. Forbes, *Local authority archive services 1992* (British Library R&D Report 6090, HMSO, 1993); *Archive service statistics ... estimates* (published annually by CIPFA); S.J. Davies, *A review of the role of the county archive services and the National Library of Wales in supporting the resource needs of history in the national curriculum in Wales* (Aberystwyth, 1993); V. Gray, 'The county record office: the unfolding of an idea', in K. Neale (ed.), *An Essex tribute: essays presented to Frederick G Emmison* (1987), pp.11-25; D. Rimmer, 'Record office or local studies centre?', in *Journal of the Society of Archivists* 13, no. 1 (Spring 1992), pp.9-17; J.R. Sewell, 'Municipal archives in the United Kingdom', in *Janus* 1990.2, pp.82-87.

28. *Challenge or threat. England's archive heritage and the future of local government* (a leaflet published jointly by the National Council on Archives, the Society of Archivists and the Association of County Archivists, 1992).

29. Volume 1, HMSO, 1996. Volume 2 in preparation.

30. See R.J.Olney, 'The Portland papers', in *Archives* xix, no.82 (Oct 1989), pp.78-87.

31. *Annual report of the PRO of Northern Ireland 1990-91*, p.8.

32. ed. J. Foster and J. Sheppard (3rd edn, 1995).

33. *Directory of corporate archives* (3rd edn, 1992).

34. *Location register of twentieth-century English literary manuscripts and letters* (British Library, 2 vols., 1988). *Location register of English literary manuscripts and letters. Eighteenth and nineteenth centuries* (British Library, 2 vols., 1995).

35. Royal Historical Society, Guides and Handbooks 18 (1994).

36. *National Museum of Photography, Film and Television: the book* (1989).

37. Annual report of the West Yorkshire Archive Service 1994, p.8.

38. *Private papers of British diplomats 1782-1900* (HMSO for the Royal Commission on Historical Manuscripts, 1985), pp.41-43.

39. National Heritage Memorial Fund, *Annual report 1993/94.*

Illustrations

Cover: two illustrations from a survey of the possessions of Thomas, late duke of Norfolk and Philip, late Earl of Arundel, 31 Elizabeth I (E164/46). *Public Record Office. Crown copyright.*

1. Paper repair. *Birmingham City Archives.*
2. Section accompanying a report on Mold lead mines, Flintshire, 1827 (D/DM/219/92). *Clwyd Record Office.*
3. Photograph from an album of Cannock Chase and neighbourhood, 1892: Stafford waterworks: trial sinking at Milford (5234). *Staffordshire Record Office.*
4. Page from a bell-ringers' peal book. *Ancient Society of College Youths.*
5. James Melville's diary, 1574 with the first known archival reference to golf (Adv. MS. 34.4.15 p.25). *Trustees of the National Library of Scotland.*
6. 'The icnography of Merthir Furnace', 1763 from the Dowlais Iron Company archive (D/DQP/1/1). *Glamorgan Record Office, Cardiff.*
7. Denbigh charter, 1510 (BD/A/807). *Clwyd Record Office.*
8. Grant of arms to the Coach and Coach Harness Makers' Company, 1677 (Ms 6237). *Guildhall Library, London, Manuscripts Section and Worshipful Company of Coachmakers and Coach Harness Makers.*
9. Fragment of a medieval world map, c.1220, discovered in the binding of a volume in the archives. *Duchy of Cornwall.*
10. Family history day at Huddersfield. *West Yorkshire Archives Service.*
11. Young historians' day. *Sheffield Archives.*
12. Pedigree roll of the Gwyn family of Llansannor, c.1615 (D/D XW). *Glamorgan Record Office, Cardiff.*
13. Hearth tax money collected in Lochrutton parish, 1694 (E69/14/1). *Scottish Record Office.*
14. The search room at Canterbury cathedral archives. *Dean and Chapter of Canterbury.*
15. The first Winchester Pipe Roll, 1208-09 (11M59/B1/1). *Hampshire Record Office.*
16. Repairing fire damaged archives. *Dean and Chapter of Canterbury.*
17. Order to pay Viscount Doncaster's expenses as an ambassador to the princes of Germany in the early stages of the Thirty Years' War, from the papers of Sir William Herrick (1562-1653), teller of the Exchequer. These official papers remained in private hands and are now MS. Eng. hist.c.1297 fo 202r in the *Bodleian Library, Oxford.*
18. A register of acts of the Commissioners in Causes Ecclesiastical (The 'High Commission') for the years 1631-33, which has long been separated from the other surviving act books in the PRO (MS. Dd.2.21 fo.72r). *Cambridge University Library.*
19. Log book of Tonna Mixed School, 1874. *West Glamorgan County Archive Service.*
20. Pedigree of Lord Selsey. *British Records Association. Photograph by Belinda Syme.*
21. A solicitor's basement, early 1980s (S 22/2). *Wigan Archives Service.*
22. Aerial view of Hampshire Record Office, Winchester. *Hampshire Record Office.*
23. Scottish Record Office, Thomas Thomson House. *Scottish Record Office.*
24. Westminster Archives Centre. *Westminster City Archives.*
25. Preparing papers for press release day under the thirty year rule. *Public Record Office, Crown Copyright.*
26. Page from Lloyd George's diary, 1886. *National Library of Wales.*
27. Drawing register from the Darlington Works of the North Eastern Railway, 1918, recording incidentally the signing of the Armistice ending the First World War. *National Railway Museum, York.*
28. Daily working notes of Dick Etheridge, senior convenor at the Austin Motor Co, August 1949 (MSS 202/S/J/8). *Modern Records Centre. M.G. Gould ABIPP, University of Warwick Photographic Service.*
29. Missionary at work. The Revd C.G. Sparham of the London Missionary Society, at work probably in Hankow where he was stationed from 1885 to 1917. *School of Oriental and African Studies, London University.*
30. Accounts of collectors for the poor for the parish of St Margaret's Westminster, 14 Elizabeth I (E147). *Westminster City Archives.*
31. Grant to the Benedictine priory of Tywardreath, Cornwall, of properties in Otterham parish, early 12th century (Arundell Papers). *Cornwall Record Office.*
32. Barrett-Lennard travelling estate office. *Essex Record Office.*
33. A private muniment room in Scotland. *National Register of Archives, Scotland.*
34. Papal bull to Paisley abbey, 13th century (Abercorn papers, D623/B/7/1/1). *PRO of Northern Ireland.*
35. Magna Carta 1215. One of four surviving examples. *Dean and Chapter of Salisbury.*
36. Racking book of Highland Distillers, 1935/36

(UG 0217/15/7). *Glasgow University Archives Business Records Centre.*

37. Advertisement for the Wrexham Lager Beer Co Ltd *c.*1900 (DD/DM/456/1). *Clwyd Record Office.*
38. Railway bond of the Midi Railway Company,1922. *Rothschild Archives.*
39. The University of Warwick Library extension, housing the Modern Records Centre and BP Archive. *M.G. Gould ABIPP, University of Warwick Photographic Service.*
40. Poster attributed to 'Mansbridge' from the vintage year 1932. *BP Archives.*
41. Captain Eyston achieved this record breaking feat in his 21,236cc 12 cylinder Rolls-Royce aero-engined 'Speed of the Wind' in 1935. *BP Archives.*
42. Coloured drawings by John Leighe, 1598, recording the glass then in All Saints Church, Northampton. *Northamptonshire Record Office.*
43. Handel autograph of an air 'composed at St Giles by Mr Handel extempore, & afterwards by desire of the company writt down in his own hand writing as above' (Malmesbury Collection 9M73/703). *Hampshire Record Office.*
44. Plan of Brighton, 1773, drawn from memory by William Green of Lewes, showing areas washed away by the sea (AMS 6279). *East Sussex Record Office.*
45. Map used by Major-General Archdale Wilson who commanded the besieging forces at the capture of Delhi, September 1857 (6807-139). *The Director, National Army Museum.*
46. Buff Bill's Circus, c.1910 (Herbert Cooper collection, D1422/B/17/38). *Deputy Keeper of the Records, PRO of Northern Ireland.*
47. Forth rail bridge under construction *c.*1887. *Aberdeen University Library, George Washington Wilson Collection.*

48. Multi-media presentation. *Birmingham City Archives, Charles Parker Archive.*
49. National Video Archive of Stage Performance. *Theatre Museum.*
50. Fairground art from the archive of Ernest Barrett of Derby (d.1948) (D4060/1/1). *Derbyshire Record Office.*
51. Character jug pattern book. *Royal Doulton.*
52. Conservation studio, Leicestershire Record Office. *Leicestershire Museums, Arts and Records Service.*
53. Damaged archives undergoing humidification. *Dean and Chapter of Canterbury.*
54. Plan showing the order of sailing of the Dutch fleet which brought William of Orange and his commanders to England in 1688 (Pw A 2197). *Nottingham University Library, Department of Manuscripts and Special Collections* (Portland Collection).
55. John Evelyn's diary. The autograph manuscripts begin with an account of his birth in 1620 and the entries continue until a few weeks before his death in 1706. Purchased 1995. *British Library.*
56. James Watt's copying press patent of 1780. *Birmingham City Archives.*
57. Letters patent of Richard III to Esholt priory,1485. *West Yorkshire Archive Service.*
58. The Clifford Papers relating to the Secret Treaty of Dover (now in the British Library). *Reviewing Committee on the Export of Works of Art.*
59. Purcell autograph: an apparently unrecorded version of the Hornpipe from The Fairy Queen, from a unique autograph manuscript of keyboard music by Henry Purcell (Music Library Deposit 95/2 fo 5v). Acquired 1995. *British Library.*

Appendix
Organisations referred to in the text

THE NATIONAL COUNCIL ON ARCHIVES

The Council was formed in 1988 as a forum in which the interests of owners, custodians and users of archives in the United Kingdom could be represented and openly discussed, and matters of common concern be brought to the attention of the public, the government or relevant institutions.

Further information is obtainable from the Hon Secretary, NW Kingsley, Birmingham Central Library, Archives Division, Chamberlain Square, Birmingham B3 3HQ.

See Rosemary Dunhill, 'The National Council on Archives: its role in professional thinking and development', in *Journal of the Society of Archivists* 11, nos 1&2 (January and April 1990).

Members

(a) Professional bodies

Association of County Archivists
Contact: Dr Margaret O'Sullivan, Derbyshire Record Office, Education Department, County Offices, Matlock DE4 3AG.

Society of Archivists
Contact: The Executive Secretary, Society of Archivists, Information House, 20-24 Old Street, London EC1V 0AP.

Standing Conference of National and University Libraries
Contact: Michael S-M Hannon, University Library, Sheffield S10 2TN.

Cyngor Archifau Cymru/Archives Council Wales (estd 1995)
CAC/ACW brings together institutions and organisations involved in the administration of archives in Wales. It seeks to influence policy with regard to archives in Wales and to publicise matters of current concern.

Contact: Gwyn Jenkins, National Library of Wales, Aberystwyth SY23 3BU.

(b) Local authority associations:

Association of County Councils
Association of Metropolitan Authorities

(c) Bodies whose membership is open to the public:

British Association for Local History
BALH is the national organisation which represents the interests of local historians. It arranges conferences and visits and has a flourishing programme of publications. Membership is open to all on payment of an annual subscription.

Publications: *The Local Historian* and *Local History News* (both quarterly), and practical handbooks on reading and interpreting the sources for local history. The Association is a registered charity.

Contact: The administrator, Michael Cowan, 24 Lower Street, Harnham, Salisbury SP2 8EY.

British Records Association (estd 1932)
The BRA is a charitable organisation dedicated to the dissemination of information about archives and their preservation. It is the only national organisation directly concerned with archives which is open equally to owners, custodians and researchers. It seeks to develop informed public opinion on the continued preservation of records, to defend the principle of free public access to records, and to promote their use through publication. The BRA's Records Preservation Section rescues records of interest which might be at risk of destruction, particularly from the offices of London solicitors, and distributes them to appropriate custodians. The Association holds an annual conference.

Publications: *Archives*, the Association's journal

published twice yearly. *Archives and the User* series provides comprehensive introductions to particular groups of records or to archive-related research. Newsletter. Annual report. *Jubilee essays: The British Records Association 1932-1992*. Leaflets on records preservation.

Contact: The Hon Secretary, British Records Association, 18 Padbury Court, London E2 7EH.

Business Archives Council (estd 1934)

The BAC aims to encourage the preservation of the historical records of British industry and commerce and the study of Britain's industrial and commercial history. Membership is open to all. The BAC's Business Records Advisory Service surveys and rescues records at risk and where appropriate advises on their future management and storage. The Council maintains a specialist library at its headquarters and arranges an annual conference as well as training seminars.

Publications: *Business Archives* (twice yearly). Quarterly Newsletter. Conference proceedings. Surveys including the series of *Studies in British business archives* (Manchester University Press). *Record aids. Managing business archives*, etc.

Contact: The General Secretary, Business Archives Council, The Clove Building, 4 Maguire Street, London SE1 2NQ.

Federation of Family History Societies (estd 1974)

FFHS aims to coordinate and assist the work of societies or other bodies interested in family history, genealogy and heraldry, and to foster mutual cooperation and regional projects in these subjects. Membership is open to any society or body specialising in family history or an associated discipline (currently some 150 societies throughout the world including national, regional and one-name groups). National projects have included the compilation of marriage indexes for the period 1754-1837 and the transcription and indexing of the 1851 and 1881 censuses, in both cases on a county basis.

Publications: *Family History News & Digest* (twice yearly) and numerous publications on family history research and the whereabouts of relevant records. FFHS maintains a reference collection of books and periodicals at its headquarters.

Contact : The Administrator, Federation of Family History Societies, c/o Benson Room, Birmingham and Midland Institute, Margaret Street, Birmingham B3 3BS.

Historical Association (estd 1906)

The HA was founded to develop public interest in history and to advance its study at all levels. Membership is open to all interested in history, whether as amateurs or experts. The Association's numerous activities, which offer the opportunity to explore history, including local history, in a friendly and informal atmosphere, include visits, lectures and conferences (including Education conferences of special interest to teachers, and Sixth Form conferences). They are organised partly by its headquarters and partly by over 70 local branches. The Association also sponsors a wide range of publications on all aspects of history, and frequently includes items concerning archives.

Publications: *The Historian* (quarterly). *History. Primary History. Teaching History. Short Guides to Records. Annual bulletin of historical literature.* Pamphlets on many historical topics.

Contact: The Association Secretary, Historical Association, 59a Kennington Park Road, London SE11 4JH.

Royal Historical Society (estd 1868, incorporated by Royal Charter 1889)

The Society is the principal learned body for the study of history. The Fellowship is open to academic and other historians who have published substantial historical works and are recommended by other Fellows and proposed by the Society's Council for election. Membership is open to all with a professional interest in the study of history. The Society's main function is to promote the study of history through lectures, conferences and publications, and by maintaining a specialist library. Increasingly in recent years it has also acted as a pressure group representing the interests of history and historians.

Publications: *Transactions*, Camden series of edited texts, *Guides and Handbooks, Annual bibliography, Studies in History* series.

Contact: The Executive Secretary, Royal Historical Society, University College London, Gower Street, London WC1E 6BT.

Scottish Records Association (estd 1977)

The SRA fulfils a rôle complementary in some respects to that of the British Records Association, which has no regional base in Scotland. It too is open equally to owners, custodians and researchers, and seeks to create an enlightened public opinion and promote the interchange of views on matters affecting archives. It arranges conferences and visits, and disseminates information about sources. Membership is open to individuals on payment of an annual subscription.

Publications: Newsletters, Datasheets (summary lists of local record holdings) and a new journal *Scottish Archives*, incorporating conference papers as well as other articles on documentary sources for Scottish historical studies. *Scottish handwriting 1500-1700: a self-help pack*.

Contact: Dr T Clarke, Secretary, Scottish Records Association, c/o Scottish Record Office, HM General Register House, Edinburgh EH1 3YY.

(d) Organisations with observer status:

Advisory Council on Public Records
(estd 1959)

Members of the Advisory Council are appointed by the Lord Chancellor under section 1 (2) of the Public Records Act 1958, to advise him on matters concerning Public Records in general, and in particular on those aspects of the work of the PRO which affect members of the public who make use of its facilities. The Chairman, *ex officio*, is the Master of the Rolls.

Publication: Annual report, published under the same cover as the *Annual report of the Keeper of Public Records*.

Contact: Robert Wright, Secretary to the Advisory Council on Public Records, Lord Chancellor's Department, Trevelyan House, 30 Great Peter Street, London SW1 2BY.

British Library

Contact: The Director of Special Collections, The British Library, Great Russell Street, London WC1B 3DG.

Public Record Office

Contact: The Keeper, Public Record Office, Kew, Richmond, Surrey, TW9 4DU.

Royal Commission on Historical Manuscripts

Contact: The Secretary, Royal Commission on Historical Manuscripts, Quality House, Quality Court, Chancery Lane, London WC2A 1HP.

Public Record Office of Northern Ireland

Contact: The Director, Public Record Office of Northern Ireland, 66 Balmoral Avenue, Belfast BT9 6NY.

OTHER RELEVANT ORGANISATIONS

Organisations mentioned in this book, but which are not members of the National Council on Archives, include:

Association for Manuscripts and Archives in Research Collections

Founded in 1992 in succession to the SCONUL Advisory Committeee on Manuscripts, AMARC brings together the curators and users of manuscripts, archives and special collections in the national and university libraries and repositories. Membership is open to individuals and institutions on payment of an annual subscription. The Association organises occasional seminars, and members receive a twice-yearly newsletter.

Contact: Dr Ian Doyle, Durham University Library, Palace Green, Durham DH1 3RN.

Business Archives Council of Scotland
(estd 1960)

BAC Scotland is separate from, but maintains close links with, the Business Archives Council. It has similar objectives, and has been particularly active in surveying and rescuing business records and steering them into appropriate repositories. Membership is open to all.

Publications: *Scottish Industrial History* (annual).

Contact: BAC (Scotland) c/o Glasgow University Archives, Glasgow G12 8QQ.

Friends of the National Libraries (estd 1931)

The Friends help to acquire for the nation printed books, manuscripts and archives, in particular those which might otherwise leave the country.

In over 60 years they have made grants to more than 250 institutions including national and unversity libraries and county record offices. In 1993 the Friends made their largest ever grant, of £50,000 towards the purchase by Hertfordshire Record Office of the Panshanger Papers. Membership is open to all.

Publications: Annual report.

Contact: The Secretary, Friends of the National Libraries, c/o The British Library.

Historic Houses Archivists Group

Contact: Colin Shrimpton, Estate Office, Alnwick Castle, Alnwick NE66 1NQ.

National Manuscripts Conservation Trust

Contact: Mrs Stephanie Kenna, British Library Research and Development Department, 2 Sheraton Street, London W1V 4BH.

Reviewing Committee on the Export of Works of Art

Contact: Simon Mitchell, Department of National Heritage, 2-4 Cockspur Street, London SW1Y 5DH.

Index

Numbers in **bold** type refer to illustrations. Other references are to pages.